New Daylight

KU-030-009

Edited by Naomi Starkey   September–December 2010

Suggestions for using *New Daylight*

Find a regular time and place, if possible, where you can read and pray undistracted. Before you begin, take time to be still and perhaps use the BRF prayer. Then read the Bible passage slowly (try reading it aloud if you find it over-familiar), followed by the comment. You can also use *New Daylight* for group study and discussion, if you prefer.

The prayer or point for reflection can be a starting point for your own meditation and prayer. Many people like to keep a journal to record their thoughts about a Bible passage and items for prayer. In *New Daylight* we also note the Sundays and some special festivals from the Church calendar, to keep in step with the Christian year.

New Daylight and the Bible

New Daylight contributors use a range of Bible versions, and you will find a list of the versions used in each issue at the back of the notes on page 154. You are welcome to use your own preferred version alongside the passage printed in the notes, and this can be particularly helpful if the Bible text has been abridged.

New Daylight affirms that the whole of the Bible is God's revelation to us, and we should read, reflect on and learn from every part of both Old and New Testaments. Usually the printed comment presents a straight-forward 'thought for the day', but sometimes it may also raise questions rather than simply providing answers, as we wrestle with some of the more difficult passages of Scripture.

New Daylight is also available in a deluxe edition (larger format). Check out your local Christian bookshop or contact the BRF office, who can also give more details about a cassette version for the visually impaired. For a Braille edition, contact St John's Guild, 8 St Raphael's Court, Avenue Road, St Albans, AL1 3EH.

Writers in this issue

Margaret Silf is an ecumenical Christian, committed to working across and beyond the denominational divides. She devotes herself to writing and accompanying others on their spiritual journey.

Jennifer Oldroyd worked for many years at the Ashburnham Place conference centre in East Sussex. In the last few years she has had published two books of study material for small groups.

Rachel Boulding is Deputy Editor of the Church Times. Previously, she was Senior Liturgy Editor at Church House Publishing. She lives in Dorset with her husband and son.

Tony Horsfall is a freelance trainer and retreat leader based in Yorkshire, with his own ministry, Charis Training. He has written several books for BRF, most recently Working from a Place of Rest.

Naomi Starkey is the Editor of New Daylight, as well as commissioning BRF's books for adults. She has also written Pilgrims to the Manger, BRF's 2010 Advent book, and Good Enough Mother (BRF, 2009). She is married to Mike, an Anglican vicar, and they have three children.

John Proctor works for the United Reformed Church, teaching the New Testament to students in Cambridge and church groups around the UK. John has written The People's Bible Commentary: Matthew (BRF, 2001).

Stephen Rand is a writer and speaker who, in recent years, has shared his time between Jubilee Debt Campaign, persecuted church charity Open Doors and Mainstream, a Baptist church leaders' network.

David Robertson has ministered in a variety of parishes since his ordination in 1979 and is currently a vicar in Halifax. He has written Marriage—Restoring Our Vision and Collaborative Ministry for BRF.

Elaine Duncan is the Chief Executive of the Scottish Bible Society, which supports Bible translation, production and distribution around the world and encourages engagement with the Bible in Scotland.

Amy Boucher Pye is an American who has lived in the UK for over a decade. She makes her home in North London with her husband and young family and enjoys writing for Christian periodicals, including Quiet Spaces, Woman Alive and Christian Marketplace.

Further BRF reading for this issue

For more in-depth coverage of some of the passages in these Bible reading notes, we recommend the following titles:

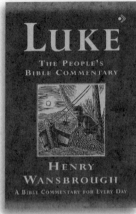

LUKE
THE PEOPLE'S BIBLE COMMENTARY

HENRY WANSBROUGH
A BIBLE COMMENTARY FOR EVERY DAY

978 1 84101 027 4, £7.99

1 & 2 KINGS
THE PEOPLE'S BIBLE COMMENTARY

STEPHEN B. DAWES
A BIBLE COMMENTARY FOR EVERY DAY

978 1 84101 118 9, £7.99

ISAIAH
THE PEOPLE'S BIBLE COMMENTARY

JO BAILEY WELLS
A BIBLE COMMENTARY FOR EVERY DAY

978 1 84101 151 6, £8.99

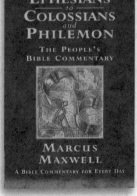

EPHESIANS
to
COLOSSIANS
and
PHILEMON
THE PEOPLE'S BIBLE COMMENTARY

MARCUS MAXWELL
A BIBLE COMMENTARY FOR EVERY DAY

978 1 84101 047 2, £7.99

Naomi Starkey writes...

When we read the Bible, it is always good to do so with an eye on 'the big picture'. Yes, God can speak to us personally through the passage we read; yes, we can find unexpected and powerful insights for our individual lives and lessons to apply in our journey of discipleship, but we should not forget that the Bible is not just about us, here and now. Of course God loves and cares about each one of us, but we are also part of a vast, eternal story that we will only understand when we are finally in his presence.

At the same time, parts of the Bible that may seem of limited application to the 21st century can still be a means of teaching us more about God's purposes for the world. In our continuing series of 'Bible stories rediscovered', Stephen Rand writes on Noah, covering not only the flood and the ark but also the shameful episode that followed. He shows how that narrative can teach us far more than we might assume, given the ark's traditional status as a highlight of children's picture Bibles (as is true for so many of our 'Bible stories rediscovered'!).

It's good to be able to welcome Elaine Duncan of the Scottish Bible Society, who has written some readings on the letters to the 'seven churches of Asia' found in the opening chapters of the book of Revelation. While many people find this a difficult part of scripture, Elaine points out in her introduction that it nevertheless 'encourages us to see our lives in the bigger context of God's rule and reign in the world and across the ages'.

For me, however, the highlight of this issue of *New Daylight* are Rachel Boulding's beautifully written and inspiring readings on 'words of commitment'—God's commitment to us and (as she puts it) 'our more faltering commitment to him'. Over seven days of notes, which she wrote in the breathing space between chemotherapy sessions for cancer, she explores how God's love for his creation is both the foundation and the furthest limit of the 'big picture'. On 27 September, she summarises this in a single pithy sentence: 'Our purpose is love: to be loved, to love and to spread God's love.'

The BRF Prayer

Almighty God,
you have taught us that your word is a lamp for our feet
and a light for our path. Help us, and all who prayerfully
read your word, to deepen our fellowship with each other
through your love. And in so doing may we come to know you more
fully, love you more truly, and follow more faithfully in
the steps of your son Jesus Christ, who lives and reigns with
you and the Holy Spirit, one God for evermore. Amen.

Snapshots of Jesus: Luke

I enjoy photography—or perhaps it would be more accurate to say that I enjoy taking snapshots because, whatever my 'photography' is, it is certainly not very expert. I could show you many snaps of 'things that got away', from a spectacular puffin that vacated a clump of Scottish grass just before my shutter clicked to a whole school of whales that vanished at the crucial moment in South African waters. Perhaps my most inept attempt was one day when I was walking on a Welsh hillside and heard what sounded like a ton of breakfast cereal snap-crackle-and-popping as if a lake of milk had just been poured over it. On investigation I found that the power of the sun that morning was just right to cause the furze bushes to pop their seedcases en masse, giving rise to this Hallelujah chorus. I took a snapshot of the event, which, in retrospect, was very silly as it didn't amount to much without the audio effects.

The truth is that our photos will always fall way short of the reality. At best they can only remind us of past events and experiences and invite us to go back to them and renew our joy in them. So why would I try to take 'snapshots' of Jesus? Well, I guess for the same reason that I take other snapshots—because I love the subjects so much that I don't want to be without a reminder of them. So it is for this reason that I wander through the events of the Gospels (in this case the Gospel of Luke) with an eye open for what especially attracts my attention. In doing so, I will certainly walk past a thousand other incidents, equally momentous. All I can do is share with you the special moments that have spoken to me in my journey with Luke and invite you to discover what they mean for you.

If the reality of our world consistently evades our cameras, how much more will the mystery of God elude our attempts to express it? Even so, our snapshots matter. They are reminders of what has touched our hearts. So, I wish you God's blessing as you browse this little album from Luke. May it take you a little deeper into the heart of the one who is closer to you than you are to yourself.

Margaret Silf

Straight talker

And the crowds asked him, 'What then should we do?' In reply he said to them, 'Whoever has two coats must share with anyone who has none; and whoever has food must do likewise.' Even tax-collectors came to be baptised, and they asked him, 'Teacher, what should we do?' He said to them, 'Collect no more than the amount prescribed for you.' Soldiers also asked him, 'And we, what should we do?' He said to them, 'Do not extort money from anyone by threats or false accusation, and be satisfied with your wages.'

It is sometimes said, 'If you don't think you will like the answer, don't ask the question.' Today everyone plies Jesus with a question: the crowds, the tax-collectors, even the soldiers. The question they ask is simple: 'What should we do?' Jesus' answer is as simple and direct as their question and it carries just the same weight today for us: do the right thing by your fellow human beings. Share what you have with those in need. Be just in your dealings with each other. Don't use force to threaten people, even the subtle force of dishonest suggestion or emotional pressure. Be content in your own hearts.

I wonder if the questioners liked what they heard. Quite possibly they nodded approvingly and then went on living the way they had always lived. The implications of Jesus' straight talking are much more far-reaching, much more disturbingly uncomfortable, than most of us really want to contemplate. Perhaps they went away wishing they had never asked!

What about ourselves? We might well include this same question in our prayers: what then should I do? Do we want to hear Jesus' answer? Are we willing to hear what he is suggesting in our hearts, above the noise of what we ourselves want to do? The two may not always be the same. When we look honestly at the particular situations in our own lives, and in the life of our world right now, what straight answers might Jesus be wanting to give us?

Reflection

Ask an honest question and Jesus will give you a straight answer. Dare you,
dare we, pose the question, 'What then should we do?'

MS

A man who can't be silenced

When they heard this, all in the synagogue were filled with rage. They got up, drove him out of the town, and led him to the brow of the hill on which their town was built, so that they might hurl him off the cliff. But he passed through the midst of them and went on his way. He went down to Capernaum, a city in Galilee, and was teaching them on the sabbath. They were astounded at his teaching, because he spoke with authority.

The town from which Jesus has been driven out is his own home town of Nazareth, and his comment on the violent antagonism of his fellow Nazarenes is that no prophet is accepted in his own country (v. 24). They are not exactly subtle in expressing their dislike of the home truths Jesus gives them. He has been reminding them of other times and examples of how God's chosen ones had blocked the power of his love and healing through their own resistance. On hearing these unpalatable truths, they turn on him and hound him out of town. Those who had applauded his wisdom just moments earlier now drive him away in their murderous rage.

We learn, however, that he 'passed through the midst of them and went on his way.' This is a man who has nothing to prove. He is who he is. He has no need to justify his claims to anyone or defend himself against the hostility of these people, because he speaks with the ultimate authority—the authority that comes from the author of all being. Yet that same powerful authority provokes their defences and rouses their fury. The darkness will not tolerate the light of truth.

Empowered by this, the only authority that has true value, Jesus moves on to Capernaum to speak to more receptive hearts. Truth will not, and cannot, be silenced and this man is the Truth; his light will never be suppressed by the force of darkness.

We too can be guilty of muffling God's truth to suit ourselves. Where will our own hearts rest: in 'Nazareth' or 'Capernaum'?

Reflection

In what subtle ways do we, Jesus' 'own people', in the 21st century, also sometimes try to silence his truth?

MS

Challenger of the rules

One sabbath while Jesus was going through the cornfields, his disciples plucked some heads of grain, rubbed them in their hands, and ate them. But some of the Pharisees said, 'Why are you doing what is not lawful on the sabbath?' Jesus answered, 'Have you not read what David did when he and his companions were hungry? He entered the house of God and took and ate the bread of the Presence, which it is not lawful for any but the priests to eat, and gave some to his companions?' Then he said to them, 'The Son of Man is lord of the sabbath.'

I'll never forget the day I left my childhood home to live and work abroad. After a tearful farewell, I climbed on board a train—the wrong train! This train was headed south-west; I needed to go to an airport in the south-east of the country. As soon as I realised my mistake, I looked for the train manager to ask his advice. He could have insisted on my paying the fare to somewhere I didn't want to go and sitting out the unwanted journey reflecting on my missed flight. Instead, he contacted the driver of the train I should have been on. To my amazement, both express trains made an unscheduled stop at a tiny village along the common part of their route and so I sheepishly crossed the platform, leaving the wrong train and getting on to the right train.

I remember that kindness to this day and thank God for two people who were willing to break the rules to enable me to continue my journey, just as Jesus does for his friends in today's snapshot.

Challenged by the Pharisees on the minor infringement of plucking a grain of wheat on the sabbath when walking through a cornfield, Jesus responds by drawing their attention to an apparently much more serious infringement by King David and how the imperative of human hunger overrides any man-made rules. He is constantly striving to help us move on in our journey with God, keeping the focus on what is important, not on our rules.

Reflection

Do you feel that any man-made 'rule' is obstructing your journey with God? What do you think the Lord of the sabbath would advise you to do?

MS

A man who can smile

He also told them a parable: 'Can a blind person guide a blind person? Will not both fall into a pit? A disciple is not above the teacher, but everyone who is fully qualified will be like the teacher. Why do you see the speck in your neighbour's eye, but do not notice the log in your own eye?' Or how can you say to your neighbour, "Friend, let me take out the speck in your eye", when you yourself do not see the log in your own eye? You hypocrite, first take the log out of your own eye, and then you will see clearly to take the speck out of your neighbour's eye.'

'Laughter is the best medicine.' As we now know, this isn't just a bit of folk wisdom; it is a verifiable scientific fact. I have a friend with whom I spend a couple of weeks' holiday every year and she has an amazing ability to make me laugh—laugh with my whole being. Those two weeks set me up for the whole year.

Laughter, we now know, reduces stress and relieves pain, strengthens our immune systems and helps us to relax by day and sleep at night. So why would we think that Jesus, the greatest healer who ever walked the earth, went around being solemn and serious all the time, as too many of us, his followers, tend to do in the context of faith practice?

This parable is surely an example of Jesus at his tongue-in-cheek best. He exaggerates the scene so completely that even his most hostile opponents could surely not have failed to notice the twinkle in his eye at the image of the infamous 'log' in the eye of the overly zealous critic. We have all met such people. Jesus invites us to laugh with him—not so much at them, but at ourselves. In a nutshell, perhaps, he might be inviting us to take God seriously, but to take ourselves and our self-importance lightly!

In Jesus' teaching, more often than we realise perhaps, a dash of laughter certainly makes the medicine go down.

Reflection
Reflect tonight on what has made you laugh during the day, and thank God for the gift of a sense of humour.

MS

11

Comforter of the afflicted

Soon afterwards he went to a town called Nain, and his disciples and a large crowd went with him. As he approached the gate of the town, a man who had died was being carried out. He was his mother's only son, and she was a widow; and with her was a large crowd from the town. When the Lord saw her, he had compassion for her and said to her, 'Do not weep.' Then he came forward and touched the bier, and the bearers stood still. And he said, 'Young man, I say to you, rise!' The dead man sat up and began to speak, and Jesus gave him to his mother.

When I reflect upon this tender and beautiful incident, I see the compassion of Jesus flowing like a river. In this instance, the source of the river lies in his deep heart-connection to the anguish of this passing stranger, a woman on her way to bury her only son. In today's snapshot, I see a man walking along the road, going about his business, teaching and guiding the crowd that follows him, but pausing to attend to the grief of just one single person along the way, noticing the need of the individual among the multitude.

The river of Jesus' love enfolds this one, finding expression in his words of comfort: 'Do not weep.' It flows on into his actions as he reaches out to touch the bier—to touch the very heart of her loss and loneliness. It then reaches its destination when Jesus gives back to the sorrowing mother the son she thought she had lost forever.

It is this flow of outpoured compassion that brings about the miracle. The focus of Jesus' words and actions remains steadfastly on the afflicted one, to whom he alone can bring comfort. Just as he notices the suffering individual among the crowd, he constantly attends to each one of us, whether we acknowledge that love or not. He is constantly reaching out to touch us, too, with the love that changes things.

Reflection

Take a few minutes to call to mind your own most grievous loss. Allow Jesus to 'touch the bier', the epicentre of your pain, letting his compassion flow into and through you.

MS

LUKE 12:49–53 (NRSV)

Afflicter of the comfortable

[Jesus said to his disciples] 'I came to bring fire to the earth, and how I wish it were already kindled! I have a baptism with which to be baptised, and what stress I am under until it is completed! Do you think that I have come to bring peace to the earth? No, I tell you, but rather division! From now on, five in one household will be divided, three against two and two against three; they will be divided: father against son and son against father, mother against daughter and daughter against mother, mother-in-law against her daughter-in-law and daughter-in-law against mother-in-law.'

The one whose love for us flows like a cooling river of compassion is also the one whose passion burns like fire. The fire of his message, as he well knows, will often flare like a living barrier between those who embrace his presence and those who resist it.

Very hard words. When I reflect on them, though, I think of the eucalypt seeds in the Australian outback, which cannot burst open and germinate until they have been exposed to the searing heat of the forest fires. I think of barren land that only becomes productive after a volcanic eruption has covered it with lava and left behind a residue of fresh nutrients and fertile soil.

In today's snapshot, Jesus reveals himself as the 'tough lover' who knows that sometimes things have to get worse before they get better and old attitudes and harmful dependencies may need to be burned away by the heat of his love for us, before new and healthy growth can begin.

Of one thing we may be sure: if this fire comes from God and is kindled by Jesus, it will ultimately be a life-giving fire, stripping away our illusions and false attachments and leaving the core of our being free to grow into the person God longs for us to be. What may appear to be destructive becomes, in God's grace, a purging of all that keeps us apart from ourselves, each other and God.

Reflection

Dare we trust the healing flame of God's fire? Dare we let it burn in our lives? Do we really believe that, however hard the challenge, God is constantly bringing us to deeper levels of love and relationship?

MS

Dweller at the heart of peace

One day he got into a boat with his disciples, and he said to them, 'Let us go across to the other side of the lake.' So they put out, and while they were sailing he fell asleep. A gale swept down on the lake, and the boat was filling with water, and they were in danger. They went to him and woke him up, shouting, 'Master, Master, we are perishing!' And he woke up and rebuked the wind and the raging waves; they ceased, and there was a calm. He said to them, 'Where is your faith?' They were afraid and amazed, and said to one another, 'Who then is this, that he commands even the winds and the water, and they obey him?'

Where is this still centre at the heart of peace? As we read the Gospels we often find Jesus in the peace of prayer in special places—on mountainsides, in a garden, in the wilderness. Today's snapshot, however, reveals the true location of that heart of peace. Jesus carries it with him, deep inside himself, through whatever befalls, including life's worst storms.

Gerard Hughes, tireless champion of justice and peace, was once asked, 'If you could ask God to bring peace to one particular place of conflict and tension in the world, which place would that be? Where is God's peace most acutely needed?' He replied, 'My own heart!'

The truth is that if we don't carry the peace of God in our own hearts, we won't find it anywhere else, however far we travel. There is only one 'special place' where the encounter with God is real and powerful and that is in each human heart. All outer peace flows from that sacred centre and spreads out to bring peace to the situations we experience.

The one who calms the waves is the same as the one who brings peace to our hearts, wherever we go, if we will only make the time and the space to go to the heart of ourselves and encounter the Lord of all peace waiting there.

Reflection

How might you be able to find ten minutes 'at the heart of peace' today? If you think it's impossible, ask the one who calmed the waters to help you.

MS

Encourager

[Jesus said to his disciples] 'Do not be afraid, little flock, for it is your Father's good pleasure to give you the kingdom. Sell your possessions, and give alms. Make purses for yourselves that do not wear out, an unfailing treasure in heaven, where no thief comes near and no moth destroys. For where your treasure is, there your heart will be also. Be dressed for action and have your lamps lit; be like those who are waiting for their master to return from the wedding banquet, so that they may open the door for him as soon as he comes and knocks.'

I took a little walk through the woods the other day. The canopy of trees, still green and dense with late summer leaves, let the sunlight through only in narrow bands, casting dappled light across the footpath and surrounding undergrowth. I noticed one tiny sapling along the wayside, literally basking in its own little pool of sunlight, soaking up everything it needed of the warmth and light and the nutrients of the soil that enabled it to grow.

In today's passage, Jesus provides just such a pool of sunlight for us—gently encouraging us with the assurance of God's own longing to give us the fullness of life and going on to show us how to prepare our hearts to receive these gifts of grace. There is, of course, a big difference between the two: the sunlight falls randomly on the tiny sapling, so other saplings may be left in the cold; the love of God, as revealed through Jesus, falls on all living beings, no one is excluded.

These words of encouragement and guidance, then, fall on our souls like the sunlight on the little sapling in the woods and enable us to grow and flourish, to become the people God created us to be. The words of affirmation are followed up not with a list of 'thou shalt nots' but positive pointers as to how we can live free of worldly anxieties and always in a state of readiness for the coming of God's grace into our lives.

Reflection

Allow yourself a little time today simply to be present to God's love falling like sunlight on your heart and your life, knowing that this love is constantly feeding the roots of your being.

MS

Storyteller

[Jesus told this parable]: 'Two men went up to the temple to pray, one a Pharisee and the other a tax-collector. The Pharisee, standing by himself, was praying thus: "God, I thank you that I am not like other people: thieves, rogues, adulterers, or even like this tax-collector. I fast twice a week; I give a tenth of all my income.' But the tax-collector, standing far off, would not even look up to heaven, but was beating his breast and saying, "God, be merciful to me, a sinner!" I tell you, this man went down to his home justified rather than the other; for all who exalt themselves will be humbled, but all who humble themselves will be exalted.'

Everyone loves a story, but no one wants to be lectured. Anyone who has ever addressed a group of people will know how their faces light up at the words, 'That reminds me of a story…' Stories strike deeper into our hearts and remain longer in our memories than lectures because they speak heart-language, not just head-language. They engage our experience and imagination, not just our brain cells.

Stories also evoke images. All of us will have a mental picture of these two men presenting themselves before God in prayer: the self-assured Pharisee and the humble, desperate tax collector. Jesus could have delivered this message in a 'sermon', warning us of the danger of self-righteousness and the need for total humility before our God. Instead, he tells us a story and paints a word-picture that none of us will forget—a story with which we can identify, finding ourselves in its characters and asking the questions of ourselves that this discovery demands. Jesus manages, in just five sentences, to say what it might have taken whole volumes of moral theology, or hour upon hour of demoralising sermons, to convey.

What does this particular story say to you? How does it leave you feeling? What picture does it engrave on your heart? Where does it resonate with our own contemporary experiences?

Reflection

Which is your favourite of Jesus' many stories? Revisit it today and notice how its meaning and power have travelled down through two millennia to strike a personal and deeply relevant chord in your heart.

MS

LUKE 7:18–23 (NRSV)

Pragmatist

John summoned two of his disciples and sent them to the Lord to ask, 'Are you the one who is to come, or are we to wait for another?' When the men had come to him, they said, 'John the Baptist has sent us to you to ask, "Are you the one who is to come, or are we to wait for another?"' Jesus had just then cured many people of diseases, plagues, and evil spirits, and had given sight to many who were blind. And he answered them, 'Go and tell John what you have seen and heard: the blind receive their sight, the lame walk, the lepers are cleansed, the deaf hear, the dead are raised, the poor have the good news brought to them. And blessed is anyone who takes no offence at me.'

'Who are you?' they ask. 'Where are you now?' we may echo. Jesus doesn't refer them to the books or the experts, but invites them—and us!—simply to open our eyes. Where do you see these things happening right now? The blind, the blinkered, the overshadowed ones being given new clarity of vision; those crippled by life's burdens being helped to move on; those ostracised by others' prejudices being welcomed in; those who have closed up against the good news of God hearing the story in fresh, engaging ways; those who thought there was nothing to live for being offered a new lease of life? 'Wherever you see these things happening, I am there', Jesus tells us.

Jesus is the supreme pragmatist—one who warns us that all our theology amounts to nothing if it isn't grounded in real, lived experience, rather than in theory and dogma. In today's snapshot I see the true son of a carpenter—the practical man who teaches us in practical ways to follow a way of life that shows practical effects. Just as he invites John's disciples to judge for themselves who he is by the fruits of what he does, so he calls us also to look around us and watch him at work in what we see.

Reflection

Where is Jesus active today, for you, in your time, your world, your street, your home, your heart?

MS

Provocative critic

[Jesus said] 'Woe to you Pharisees! For you tithe mint and rue and herbs of all kinds, and neglect justice and the love of God; it is these you ought to have practised, without neglecting the others. Woe to you Pharisees! For you love to have the seat of honour in the synagogues and to be greeted with respect in the market-places… Woe also to you lawyers! For you load people with burdens hard to bear, and you yourselves do not lift a finger to ease them…' When he went outside, the scribes and the Pharisees began to be very hostile towards him and to cross-examine him about many things, lying in wait for him, to catch him in something he might say.

I sometimes find myself thinking—and saying—that the message of Jesus is actually utterly simple, and yet incredibly difficult to live. Religious teaching and practice, on the other hand, can sometimes reverse this, making the message of Jesus appear to be very complex and difficult, while at the same time implying that, if we just 'keep the rules', it is relatively easy to live it.

Perhaps it is this kind of distortion that Jesus is challenging in today's snapshot. He is a ruthless critic of people or practices that make the journey difficult for others without lifting a finger to help them and of those who reduce the challenge of following Jesus to a set of human rules.

Let us be careful, therefore, when we catch ourselves meticulously measuring out our 'mint and rue and herbs' and donning our symbols of status and rank, as well as telling others how they should behave without lifting a finger to help them live more fully. Jesus might have hard words for *us*. It is easy to regard these things as the practices of long ago and far away, but when we allow Jesus to scratch the surface of our own practices, we may be disturbed at what we see there.

The Pharisees don't take kindly to the observations of the critical Jesus. Neither will we. When we find ourselves reacting angrily to constructive criticism, then perhaps we should be especially on our guard against our inner Pharisee.

Reflection

What do you think Jesus would challenge in the ways we practise our faith?

MS

LUKE 24:28–32 (NRSV)

Kindler of inner fire

As they came near the village to which they were going, [Jesus] walked ahead as if he were going on. But they urged him strongly, saying, 'Stay with us, because it is almost evening and the day is now nearly over.' So he went in to stay with them. When he was at the table with them, he took bread, blessed and broke it, and gave it to them. Then their eyes were opened, and they recognised him; and he vanished from their sight. They said to each other, 'Were not our hearts burning within us while he was talking to us on the road?'

Our remote ancestors, it is said, especially those who lived in cold climates and harsh terrain, would sometimes carry with them an ember of charcoal from the tribal campfire when they set off on a journey. When night fell, they would be able to rekindle this ember into a fresh fire, from which they would take another ember with them on the next stage of their journey.

Perhaps something like this is happening on the road to Emmaus, which is where this conversation occurs, as the risen Jesus walks, incognito, alongside the travellers, before revealing himself in the breaking of bread. He encourages them to talk about their recent experience in Jerusalem, of losing the one they had loved and followed, of losing heart and of being bewildered and lost in the wake of these terrible events. Then he explains to them how all this devastation was necessary, so that a greater good could be born. Then, seated in the house and sharing a meal, their eyes are opened and that nearly dead ember of faith is reignited, never again to be extinguished.

We, too, carry in our hearts an ember of our own encounters with the living God. When we meet God in prayer, in scripture, in the breaking of bread and in reflection on our own life's journey day by day, that ember is rekindled into a living fire.

Reflection

Try reading the full version of today's passage (Luke 24:13–35) and invite Jesus to open it up to you specifically in the light of your own life's path. What embers of faith might Jesus long to rekindle in your own heart and memories?

MS

Letters to Asia Minor:
Colossians and Philemon

I often wonder what Paul would write to my church if he were alive and teaching today. Paul has never visited my church, but then he never visited the church at Colosse in person either because he was actually in prison when he wrote his letter to the people there. It seems that the church had been infiltrated by religious relativism, with some believers attempting to combine elements of pagan and secular philosophy with Christian doctrine. In our own age of 'pick and mix' religion, maybe my church—and yours—needs Paul's message just as urgently.

Paul's aim was to combat the errors that had crept in and show the believers that everything they needed could be found in Christ. In his companion letter—to Philemon—he makes it clear that, in Christ, we can also find the power that makes impossible relationships possible.

Colossians is written to a young church in a city on the banks of the river Lycus in south-east Asia Minor (modern-day Turkey). Paul often comments in the letter on his readers' pagan past and it is likely that Colosse had its fair share of the many and varied religious practices that characterised the region at that time. As people moved from place to place, the lines between cults and religious ideas became blurred, so there would have been an extraordinary mixture of leftovers from the classical Greek gods, Jewish beliefs, pagan cults and the weird and wonderful ideas that flourish when men and women are hungry for spiritual reality but ignorant of the one true God.

So Paul decided to write to the believers, encouraging them and assuring them of his prayers, but determined to set them straight on the gospel path once again. Perhaps the key verse of Colossians is 2:10: 'For in [Christ] the whole fullness of deity dwells bodily, and you have come to fullness in him.' As we read Paul's message in these two letters, we need to understand and appreciate the cultural context in which they were written and open our hearts and minds to the Holy Spirit to see the application of this teaching to our own lives.

There is not room on each page to include the entire text of these letters, so some key verses have been picked out, but do try to read the letters as a whole—you will find it more than worthwhile.

Jennifer Oldroyd

COLOSSIANS 1:3–5, 9–10 (NRSV, ABRIDGED)

'We have not ceased praying for you'

In our prayers for you we always thank God... for we have heard of your faith in Christ Jesus and of the love that you have for all the saints, because of the hope laid up for you in heaven... For this reason, since the day we heard it, we have not ceased praying for you and asking that you may be filled with the knowledge of God's will in all spiritual wisdom and understanding, so that you may lead lives worthy of the Lord, fully pleasing to him, as you bear fruit in every good work and as you grow in the knowledge of God.

Wherever Paul went, he preached the gospel—and whenever people believed the message that he spoke, they were changed. Paul did not suffer from the delusion that it was his words which transformed lives and communities, though. He knew that it was the gospel 'bearing fruit and growing in the whole world' (v. 6). He also knew that having one's feet set on the right path is not the end of the story. It is necessary to progress in the right direction. That is why, in his epistles, he so often begins by assuring the Christians that he is praying for them.

Different churches—even within the same denomination—can develop different emphases, so it is vital to return to the scriptures to measure ourselves against Christ's teaching, the example of the apostles and the Holy Spirit's leading. The personal experiences of Christians in other cultures and other parts of the world can become hot news and we ask ourselves if we should expect the same. How can we know what is right for our particular part of the body of Christ?

Paul's answer was prayer—and what do we pray for in our prayer meetings, home groups and private devotional times? Next time we are responsible for leading prayer, we could try using some of Paul's prayers, in this epistle and others, so that those we pray for will always please the Lord (v. 10).

Prayer

Thank you, Father, for calling us into the kingdom of light. Watch over us and all those we love and pray for, that we may come to know you better and better. Amen

JO

'He himself is before all things'

[Christ] is the image of the invisible God, the firstborn of all creation; for in him all things in heaven and on earth were created,
things visible and invisible, whether thrones or dominions or rulers
or powers—all things have been created through him and for him.
He himself is before all things, and in him all things hold together.
He is the head of the body, the church; he is the beginning, the
firstborn from the dead, so that he might come to have first place in
everything. For in him all the fullness of God was pleased to dwell,
and through him God was pleased to reconcile to himself all things.

Paul had heard that some at Colosse were bringing into the church
teachings that were not consistent with the truth about Jesus. We only
have his responses, not the original reports, but we can deduce what
the errors were. The primary one was that Jesus could not be both
human and divine. The next was that creation is essentially evil and
only the spiritual world is good.

Right at the start of his letter, Paul sets out the truth about the
person and work of Christ. Jesus is the exact likeness of the unseen
God, Creator of the world, Lord of time and space. He is the one who
has made it possible for sinful human beings to make their peace with
Almighty God.

Paul goes on later to talk about how church members should live.
They shouldn't tell lies; they should treat everyone the same, regard-
less of standing; they should be ready to suffer, ready to forgive, ready
to love. He provides instructions for wives, husbands and children, for
masters and slaves. All that is only possible, though, if they understand
who Jesus is—for the world and for them.

Today we are blessed with an abundance of Christian teaching—sermons, books, conferences, the Internet. Is it all good? There is only one
way to judge, which is to test whether or not it preaches Christ as Lord
of all creation and the only way to God.

Prayer

*Heavenly Father, thank you for Jesus. Help us to absorb these truths about
who he is and what he has done for us. Amen*

JO

COLOSSIANS 1:24–27 (NRSV)

'The glory of this mystery'

I am now rejoicing in my sufferings for your sake, and in my flesh I am completing what is lacking in Christ's afflictions for the sake of his body, that is, the church. I became its servant according to God's commission that was given to me for you, to make the word of God fully known, the mystery that has been hidden throughout the ages and generations but has now been revealed to his saints. To them God chose to make known how great among the Gentiles are the riches of the glory of this mystery, which is Christ in you, the hope of glory.

Paul had a gift for understanding where people were in their faith journeys and how to connect with them. He has heard that, in Colosse, some were preaching that in order to be saved it was necessary to gain a certain kind of secret knowledge about the spiritual realm—knowledge only available to the select few. Some of us are still tempted in this way. We see others grow in their spiritual lives; we hear them pray and see the answers to those prayers and we are tempted to think, 'What's their secret?' So we read the books they read and search the scriptures they quote.

The truth is, there is only one secret. Paul reveals the mystery twice—first: 'Christ in you, the hope of glory' (v. 27) and then again in 2:2–3: 'Christ himself, in whom are hidden all the treasures of wisdom and knowledge.'

The 'mystery' of any growth in the Christian life, any power in prayer, any increase in faith, any demonstration of love and joy and peace is the presence of Jesus Christ in the life of the believer.

Having shared that secret with his audience, Paul explains why he has done this: 'so that no one may deceive you' (2:4). Never let anyone talk you into the 'secret of success' in the Christian life. There is only one secret, which is Jesus Christ himself, now and always.

Prayer

Lord Jesus Christ, I worship you as my only Saviour. Draw me closer to you today and share with me your treasures of wisdom and knowledge.
Amen

JO

'You have come to fullness in him'

As you therefore have received Christ Jesus the Lord, continue to live your lives in him, rooted and built up in him and established in the faith, just as you were taught, abounding in thanksgiving. See to it that no one takes you captive through philosophy and empty deceit, according to human tradition, according to the elemental spirits of the universe, and not according to Christ. For in him the whole fullness of deity dwells bodily, and you have come to fullness in him, who is the head of every ruler and authority.

Another error that had crept into the church at Colosse was that no one could be counted a believer until he or she had jumped through various hoops. We don't know what all of them were, but, from Paul's comments here, one of them was certainly circumcision.

For Jews, it was an important part of their history with God, a physical demonstration that they belonged, and so they saw it as a vital part of this new relationship with God through Christ. After the death of Christ, however, circumcision was no longer necessary. Thereafter, commitment to God is to be written on the heart. Men and women, Jews and Gentiles, children and the elderly—all can find peace with God through Christ. The proof of that new relationship with God is the death of our old nature and the growth of the new.

It still happens, of course. We may say to new Christians, 'If you really want to be a part of God's kingdom you must…', but, unless that sentence ends 'repent of your sins and believe in Jesus Christ', it is just as much an error as that being perpetrated in Colosse. We want to encourage godly living and help people put their roots down into Christ, but we cannot and must not lay on them requirements that God does not.

There is only one thing we need to say to the newly converted man or woman, alcoholic or drug addict, adulterer, thief or murderer: 'You have come to fullness in him' (v. 10).

Meditation

Christ made on the cross 'a full, perfect and sufficient sacrifice, oblation and satisfaction for the sins of the whole world'.

Service of Holy Communion, Book of Common Prayer

JO

'Don't let anyone condemn you'

Therefore do not let anyone condemn you in matters of food and drink or of observing festivals, new moons, or sabbaths. These are only a shadow of what is to come, but the substance belongs to Christ... If with Christ you died to the elemental spirits of the universe, why do you live as if you still belonged to the world? Why do you submit to regulations, 'Do not handle, Do not taste, Do not touch'? All these regulations refer to things that perish with use; they are simply human commands and teachings.

Many of us may congratulate ourselves that the legalism that had crept into the church of Colosse is not present today. We may smile at the rules churches had in the past—no alcohol, no dancing, no make-up. We may no longer condemn shopping on a Sunday or reading novels or women going hatless to church.

The error behind such attitudes is still liable to infect us, however. Paul is no fool when it comes to understanding human nature. He knows that having hard rules can make people feel good. The 'severe treatment of the body' needed in order to keep to the rules may give us a buzz, but, in fact, 'they are of no value in checking self-indulgence' (v. 23).

Jesus himself stated that true faith in God will result in fruit that can be seen (Matthew 7:20). Progress in the Christian life is not measured by how often we fast or how many prayer meetings we attend. The rules and regulations given to the people of God, and recorded in the Old Testament, were temporary, Paul says, shadows of the real thing. The real thing is Christ.

The challenge to us today is simple: are we connected to Christ (v. 19)? Are we gaining our nourishment and strength from him? Are our lives showing evidence of his Holy Spirit? Are we more loving, more joyful, more patient with people, more disciplined with ourselves? Those qualities are the only true way to measure our growth as Christians.

Prayer

Heavenly Father, help us to understand that Christ is everything for us. He is our way into your kingdom, as our Saviour, and the source of our life and strength as your children. Amen

JO

'Clothe yourselves with love'

So if you have been raised with Christ, seek the things that are above, where Christ is, seated at the right hand of God. Set your minds on things that are above, not on things that are on earth, for you have died, and your life is hidden with Christ in God... Above all, clothe yourselves with love, which binds everything together in perfect harmony. And let the peace of Christ rule in your hearts, to which indeed you were called in the one body. And be thankful. Let the word of Christ dwell in you richly; teach and admonish one another in all wisdom; and with gratitude in your hearts sing psalms, hymns, and spiritual songs to God.

Paul now urges the Christians at Colosse to compare their lives before and after Christ. Before, they strove to satisfy themselves with money, sex and power (vv. 5–10) and did not care how they achieved those things. Now they must begin to focus on Jesus. As they learn about who he is and what he has done, they will do so within the church—a community of people with similar aims and ideals. The rest of this letter consists of instructions on how to behave within that community.

In every time and place, churches exist within a particular culture, but Paul's teaching about how Christians should behave is timeless. Truth and love should mark our relationships; kindness and generosity should govern our interactions; love and forgiveness should be the basis for our dealings with others, whether within or outside the church.

If the peace of Christ rules in our hearts, we will not be easily hurt. We will not lash out when threatened or allow our egos to govern our behaviour. It is our responsibility and privilege to make sure that this is so. Of course we are constantly beset by dissension, a lack of love and a failure to put ourselves in others' shoes, but let's not give up. Instead, let's soak ourselves in these principles and, with Christ's help, begin again.

Prayer

O breath of love, come, breathe within us, renewing thought and will and heart: Come, love of Christ, afresh to win us, revive thy church in every part.

Elizabeth Porter Head (c.1914)

JO

26

'You serve the Lord Christ'

Wives, be subject to your husbands, as is fitting in the Lord. Husbands, love your wives and never treat them harshly. Children, obey your parents in everything, for this is your acceptable duty in the Lord. Fathers, do not provoke your children, or they may lose heart. Slaves, obey your earthly masters in everything… fearing the Lord. Whatever your task, put yourselves into it, as done for the Lord and not for your masters, since you know that from the Lord you will receive the inheritance as your reward; you serve the Lord Christ. For the wrongdoer will be paid back for whatever wrong has been done, and there is no partiality.

Paul wrote to real people, living in a particular place and time and culture. His instructions to them here reflect the reality of their situations, as well as the fact that the teachings of Christ were to be applied to them. The gospel should be changing every part of their lives—their marriages, parenting, working lives and so on.

This is not the place to discuss what Paul meant by wives 'being subject' to their husbands or his apparent acceptance of slavery. We need to take a long hard look at ourselves and make sure that every part of our lives is being impacted by God's grace and the Holy Spirit's power. We cannot, with impunity, be delightful Christians outside the home and act with selfish disregard for others inside it.

Here Paul says, in effect, 'You've had the Ten Commandments, telling you what not to do. Now I am telling you what, as Christians, you *should* do.' Members of the Church were never meant simply to be people who refrain from sin; we were always meant to be people who make a difference, work to change society, make disciples and demonstrate sincere love for one another.

No section of society is excluded: Paul has instructions for them all. Not just for husbands, but for wives and children, too. Not just for slaves, but for slave owners. Their faith is to govern their attitudes and actions, most intimate relationships and public faces.

Meditation

'Faith by itself, if it has no works, is dead' (James 2:17).

JO

COLOSSIANS 4:2–6 (NRSV)

'Devote yourselves to prayer'

Devote yourselves to prayer, keeping alert in it with thanksgiving. At the same time pray for us as well that God will open to us a door for the word, that we may declare the mystery of Christ, for which I am in prison, so that I may reveal it clearly, as I should. Conduct yourselves wisely towards outsiders, making the most of the time. Let your speech always be gracious, seasoned with salt, so that you may know how you ought to answer everyone.

A friend of mine was asked to join the team at church that ministers by leading worship and preaching. He has commented to me how uncomfortable he feels being at the front when so many mature believers are in the congregation. He feels that being involved in leadership implies that he is more spiritual, closer to God. In fact, this is not true. The body of Christ is just that—a body of believers, with different people playing different roles at different times.

Paul understood this and, as in so many of his letters, he finishes here with a kind of gathering in of believers. He sends greetings and words of encouragement from the brothers and sisters in one place to the brothers and sisters elsewhere (vv. 7–17) and, as always, he assures his friends of his prayers for them.

No Christian lives or ministers in isolation; we are all part of the worldwide kingdom of Jesus Christ. If, for one reason or another, you are alone today, read this last chapter of Colossians as a love letter from Paul to you. Hear his challenge to pray for those on the front line of evangelism. Take on board his instructions to share in the work of telling others about the good news. Read the greetings from these real people who laboured in the first century of Christianity and feel a fellowship with them.

Prayer

Heavenly Father, thank you for the body of Christ and for my brothers and sisters all over the world. May we rejoice in their fellowship, be faithful in prayer and take our share of the work of the kingdom, in Jesus' name.
Amen

JO

'I hear of your love'

Grace to you and peace from God our Father and the Lord Jesus Christ. When I remember you in my prayers, I always thank my God because I hear of your love for all the saints and your faith towards the Lord Jesus. I pray that the sharing of your faith may become effective when you perceive all the good that we may do for Christ. I have indeed received much joy and encouragement from your love, because the hearts of the saints have been refreshed through you, my brother.

I wonder how you would feel if a personal letter to you from a respected church leader, challenging you to a particularly difficult course of action, was made available to millions of Christians throughout the ages? Poor Philemon!

So much of scripture is personal. We read of God's dealings with individual people and the ways in which they responded. This short letter is a New Testament example of such personal application. We are studying it immediately after Colossians because it seems that Philemon was a member of that church. His home was large enough for the believers to meet in, so presumably he was fairly wealthy. He would have had a large household, including slaves. One of them, Onesimus, appears to have run away, the punishment for which is death.

Into this no doubt fairly common situation is introduced a new element: Onesimus has become a believer in Jesus, just like Philemon. On other occasions Paul has made clear his belief that new Christians should not immediately seek to change their situation in life (see, for instance, 1 Corinthians 7:20–24), so it is not surprising that he views Onesimus as still belonging to Philemon. This letter is his attempt to deal with a potentially disastrous pastoral situation.

He begins by encouraging Philemon in all that is good in his life, testifying how encouraged he has been to hear of Philemon's faith and witness and assuring him of his prayers. He particularly mentions Philemon's love—a quality that is going to be put to the test in the verses that follow.

Prayer

Lord, send us friends who will both encourage us and challenge us.

JO

'I appeal to you'

For this reason, though I am bold enough in Christ to command you to do your duty, yet I would rather appeal to you on the basis of love—and I, Paul, do this as an old man, and now also as a prisoner of Christ Jesus. I am appealing to you for my child, Onesimus, whose father I have become during my imprisonment. Formerly he was useless to you, but now he is indeed useful both to you and to me. I am sending him, that is, my own heart, back to you.

Paul has gone through incredible things for the sake of the gospel. He is currently in prison for his beliefs. Surely if anyone had the right to say, 'You must do this', it would be Paul. Instead, he appeals to Philemon on the basis of love. Paul goes on to tell how he has been instrumental in Onesimus' conversion, which has given him a love for this man that is like a father's for his son. He knows what is right to do in this situation, though, and, with a humorous play on the meaning of the slave's name, he confirms his belief that Onesimus should return to Philemon's household to live out his new faith there.

Sometimes our culture can provide similar challenges for us. In the workplace, with colleagues who have a different worldview, or in the family, perhaps with sons- or daughters-in-law with completely different backgrounds, we may find ourselves facing a Philemon moment. The obvious choice is to retreat, but this leaves no room for the grace of God.

If you are a relatively new Christian, you may have experienced many situations where you have had to work out your faith within relationships, but even if you have known Jesus for many years, you will still face challenges. How does your faith affect your relationship with others—both within and outside the Church? In answering that question we will often have to think about our attitudes, prejudices, upbringing, preferences—and the difference between what we say we believe and what we do.

Prayer

Heavenly Father, forgive us for the times when we avoid people and situations because we don't know how to deal with them. Give us the grace to find the way forward. Amen

JO

'No longer a slave but a brother'

I wanted to keep him with me... but I preferred to do nothing without your consent, in order that your good deed might be voluntary and not something forced. Perhaps this is the reason he was separated from you for a while, so that you might have him back for ever, no longer as a slave but as more than a slave, a beloved brother—especially to me but how much more to you, both in the flesh and in the Lord.

We now come to the nub of Paul's letter: Philemon is to take Onesimus back, but as a slave *and* as a Christian brother. How on earth was that going to work?

I believe one of the reasons this letter has been preserved for us is that we need to hear, in every generation and culture, that Christ has indeed broken down the walls dividing us from each other. The barriers that divide us have many names and they are high, wide and impenetrable, so we need to hear what Paul is saying here.

When we become Christians we become children of God's kingdom and inherit all that Christ purchased for us on the cross. On first understanding this truth we may rejoice in the change and eagerly set out to learn what it means in practice. When someone we consider our enemy also becomes a child of God, though? What then? How do we become brothers and sisters?

Paul has set the standard for Philemon. As an educated Jew and free-born Roman citizen, he calls a runaway slave his brother. Because he has been accepted by Jesus, despite his faults, he can now reach out in love to another human who has also been accepted by Jesus. That's all it is. Philemon must do the same. It's 'impossible', yet absolutely vital if we are truly to follow Christ.

Meditation

'For he is our peace; in his flesh he has made both groups into one and has broken down the dividing wall, that is, the hostility between us. He has abolished the law with its commandments and ordinances, so that he might create in himself one new humanity in place of the two, thus making peace' (Ephesians 2:14–15).

JO

'Refresh my heart'

So if you consider me your partner, welcome him as you would welcome me. If he has wronged you in any way, or owes you anything, charge that to my account. I, Paul, am writing this with my own hand: I will repay it. I say nothing about your owing me even your own self. Yes, brother, let me have this benefit from you in the Lord! Refresh my heart in Christ.

We may sense a certain heaviness in Paul's words here. He has battled so long and hard to reach out to men and women with the gospel. He has travelled widely, but, now that his travelling has had to cease, he is trying to continue his ministry to the new churches by letter—a long and laborious process, involving others actually doing the writing.

He has preached and written the same words over and over again: love one another, bear with one another, think of others as better than yourselves. He has received reports of petty quarrels and jealousy, of rivalry and arguments within church fellowships. Now here is yet another problem to face: an employer, a slave owner, with the law on his side, who has somehow to be convinced that his unworthy slave is now a brother in Christ. How is he going to get across what must happen?

He grabs the pen from his secretary and writes the words himself: 'It's me—Paul. Think what you owe me. Think how I have worked and prayed to save you and your slave. Think what it would mean to me to hear of you two showing to the world that master and slave can be brothers. Do it for me.'

This is the first, last and hardest lesson any of us has to learn: the lesson of love. We think we know what it means, but again and again we will be challenged. Jesus' words 'Love one another' (John 13:34–35) echo down the ages and across social divides. He continues to demand it of all of us.

Prayer

Heavenly Father, help us to love those we dislike, those we fear and those we don't understand. Give us the faith to believe that, by the work of your Holy Spirit, you can answer this prayer. Amen

JO

'The grace of the Lord Jesus Christ'

Confident of your obedience, I am writing to you, knowing that you will do even more than I say. One thing more—prepare a guest room for me, for I am hoping through your prayers to be restored to you. Epaphras, my fellow-prisoner in Christ Jesus, sends greetings to you, and so do Mark, Aristarchus, Demas, and Luke, my fellow-workers. The grace of the Lord Jesus Christ be with your spirit.

As Paul began his letter to Philemon, so he ends it—with encouragement. He assures Philemon of his belief that right will be done. He demonstrates how much he longs to be with Philemon in person and encourages him to continue to pray that this might happen. Then, as at the end of Colossians, he gathers in the others who are also praying about this situation.

Epaphras founded the church at Colosse (Colossians 1:7) and can surely be relied on to continue to pray for Philemon. Those who surrounded Paul, chronicling his activities, supporting him and praying for him, are also included in the list of those who send greetings to Philemon. This is no formulaic 'Yours sincerely' but true fellowship and a guarantee of support in prayer. Philemon would not battle alone with the challenge Paul had set him.

Finally, the grace of the Lord Jesus Christ is called down on Philemon. Only thus will he be able to do what Paul has asked. Only by the grace of God, shown in the life and death of Jesus, will we be able to rise to the challenges before us.

Relationships of all kinds provide us every day with opportunities for that grace to be at work. At home, at work, at church we will find people with whom we need to be in fellowship. Philemon is not the only one called to find a new way of interacting with someone. We too are called to take on board Paul's challenge to invest ourselves in others, relying always on the Lord Jesus Christ to enable us to do so.

Prayer

Almighty God, pour out your grace on your Church today and enable us to relate to one other with love, kindness and forbearance. Send your Holy Spirit to transform our relationships. Amen

JO

Words of commitment

This week's worth of readings look at words of commitment: God's commitment to us—full of grace and love—and our more faltering commitment to him. I have traced a path through God's covenant in Deuteronomy, which sets out obligations for both God and us, and then on to a commitment to each other (as seen with Ruth and Naomi) that we learn from God.

When we think of people being committed to each other, we usually think of marriage, so it's not surprising that the example of marriage keeps coming up in the first three readings. As ever, God shows us how strong this can be, giving us a pattern of unswerving love, rock-solid loyalty and endless forgiveness. As we will see, too, with the later readings, he doesn't just leave us an abstract ideal, but carries it through himself as our Father literally embodies it in Jesus and perseveres with it in his Holy Spirit. Then he invites us to join with him in this sharing of love. The readings later in the week go into more detail about what this entails for us.

In John's Gospel, Jesus teaches about how we can be committed to God. He emphasises the way we can live in his love, keeping his commandments. He makes a link between love and obedience, which can be hard for us to grasp at first. Jesus, however, makes it crystal clear that God is committed to us. The whole point is that God joins with us. We abide in him and he in us, in a community of love.

Now, here in this sharing, we are fed by Jesus' body and we become his body here on earth. This is the type of commitment that is a million miles away from a lonely clinging to abstract ideas or a desperate grasping at some aspiration beyond our reach.

We need to be committed; Jesus' message demands a whole-hearted response. On his side, he promises that he will always be with us. So it's not so much a strenuous effort on our part (as if we could do it all on our own), but more a sense of reflecting back something bigger than ourselves and becoming part of him. We become one with God—Father, Son and Holy Spirit—abiding in him in love.

Rachel Boulding

Sunday 26 September

DEUTERONOMY 26:17–19 (NRSV)

Keep calm and carry on—with God

Today you have obtained the Lord's agreement: to be your God; and for you to walk in his ways, to keep his statutes, his commandments, and his ordinances, and to obey him. Today the Lord has obtained your agreement: to be his treasured people, as he promised you, and to keep his commandments; for him to set you high above all nations that he has made, in praise and in fame and in honour; and for you to be a people holy to the Lord your God, as he promised.

This is God's promise to his people and our promise to him. It's a relationship of love and part of the covenant between him and humankind.

It all looks so straightforward set out like this, but, as we see throughout the Old Testament, although God is committed to us, our commitment to him is often a feeble, halting thing. The obvious question then is, 'How can we grow up and stop being squirmy, rebellious children who don't know what's good for us?' We should be mature people who flourish in the great things our Father has prepared for us.

It all becomes a bit like what we know we have to do to keep our bodies healthy: eat proper food and take some exercise. We've heard it all before and the challenge is to get on with it. Like so much of what it means to be committed to something or someone, it's not dramatic, flashy or even particularly interesting in itself: it's more a matter of persevering.

So is it all a case of dogged effort, like people in wartime, when the slogan was first dreamed up to 'Keep calm and carry on'? Surely the point is that we have much more than our own determination to fall back on. We aren't left to fight on our own, like a lonely island in battle. God helps us. God is at work within us, through his Holy Spirit. This is something that he does, not just what we do on our own.

Prayer

Go before us, Lord, in all we do with your most gracious favour, and guide us with your continual help, that in all our works begun, continued and ended in you, we may glorify your holy name.

Common Worship

RB

The Seventeenth Sunday after Trinity 35

A lifetime burning in every moment

And [Naomi] said, Behold, thy sister in law is gone back unto her people, and unto her gods: return thou after thy sister in law. And Ruth said, Entreat me not to leave thee, or to return from following after thee: for whither thou goest, I will go; and where thou lodgest, I will lodge: thy people shall be my people, and thy God my God: Where thou diest, will I die, and there will I be buried.

God's commitment to us in his covenant is strong and binding, laying the sure foundation for our life. Here, with Ruth and Naomi, we see what can be built on that rock. God's love and commitment to us create and make possible our love and commitment to each other.

One of my friends had this reading at her wedding. She knew that marriage wasn't just about delicious emotions, but about sticking with someone to the end. As my husband said, in a wonderfully matter-of-fact way, when I was diagnosed with breast cancer: 'Oh, well, in sickness and in health, love.'

Beyond the steadfast grit, is there a wider meaning? Surely the purpose of this commitment between people is to align ourselves with God's purposes, to be in tune with his ways, so that we can share his love. Our purpose is love: to be loved, to love and to spread God's love.

Commitment is a vital part of this, so that the real love isn't side-tracked into the hearts-and-flowers gush that can drain celebrations such as weddings. Commitment provides the element of continuity that ensures our affection isn't just a flash of joy—a spark of inspiration that shines out briefly, then dies away. No, this is 'a lifetime burning in every moment' (as T.S. Eliot wrote in 'East Coker' about looking back over your life).

That is why it's so healthy to begin the day by praising God. Even a minute of prayer reminds us of how God's love continues, every day, and we are part of it.

Reflection

'Beloved, since God loved us so much, we also ought to love one another. No one has ever seen God; if we love one another, God lives in us, and his love is perfected in us' (1 John 4:11).

RB

JOHN 15:9–12 (NRSV)

Love generates more love

'As the Father has loved me, so I have loved you; abide in my love. If you keep my commandments, you will abide in my love, just as I have kept my Father's commandments and abide in his love. I have said these things to you so that my joy may be in you, and that your joy may be complete. This is my commandment, that you love one another as I have loved you.'

This passage picks up on our themes of how love is shared and passed on, and the vital need for continuing commitment. It emphasises the link with keeping commandments from the Deuteronomy passage that we read on Sunday. The reason my friend had the passage from Ruth is the same as the reason my husband and I chose this passage for our wedding Gospel reading.

We need to ask why most of us struggle with the idea that love and commandments belong together. Some part of us instinctively recoils from the association between love, which is meant to be free and spontaneous, and commandments, which naturally sound forced and done only under pressure. To think like this, though, is to look at the situation the wrong way round. The Ten Commandments aren't soldiers' instructions: they are actually laws about how love works: 'Remember the sabbath day... You shall not steal' and so on. Keeping them is joining in with God's purposes of love and his plans to bring out the best in us all.

Anything else would be fighting against the way that God made the universe and the ways he works through it now (despite the efforts of his fallen creatures to spoil it). God loves us and has given us a space where we can flourish. Keeping his commandments is our loving response to his plans. If we worship other gods or covet others' goods, we're not going to be rejoicing in God's love, but if we abide in God's love (v. 10), we will find that we have kept his commandments anyway. It's a virtuous circle: if we need any tips for remaining in God, his commandments suggest some ways to behave. It's the chicken-and-egg situation we were looking at earlier—love generates more love.

Reflection
'God is love, and those who abide in love abide in God, and God abides in them' (1 John 4:16).

A golden circle of love

'No one has greater love than this, to lay down one's life for one's friends. You are my friends if you do what I command you. I do not call you servants any longer, because the servant does not know what the master is doing; but I have called you friends, because I have made known to you everything that I have heard from my Father. You did not choose me but I chose you. And I appointed you to go and bear fruit, fruit that will last, so that the Father will give you whatever you ask him in my name.'

Following on from yesterday's reading, this rightly celebrated passage is surely one of the ultimate 'words of commitment'. It has comforted millions of bereaved people with the thought that the sacrifices of the dead have not been made in vain.

It is useful to see the verse in the context of the unity of love and keeping commandments that we looked at yesterday. We can join with God in creating a community of love, remaining in his ways and being his friends. Jesus hammers home the point about it not being a case of doing what we're told: instead of being servants, we're friends; we share in what we do.

From this, we can see that it's not so much a matter of our deciding to be friends with God—as if we were to pick him out one day from a group of others—rather, he has created us, loved us and chosen a special path for us. This is a path that dovetails perfectly with the gifts God has given us and is the setting in which we can truly shine. This give-and-take is so beautifully balanced that we will bear fruit and ask him for just the right things (v. 16). We work with God in this finely tuned reciprocal sharing. It is a golden circle of commitment and love.

Reflection

The self is not lost when it is surrendered to Christ. It is lost in
a higher will, redeemed from a self-centred will, and found again
in obedience to that higher will. So it all ends in self-affirmation.
The self is not cancelled—it is heightened.

E. Stanley Jones, *The Word Became Flesh* (Abingdon, 1963)

RB

JOHN 6:53–56 (NRSV)

Sustained by his body

Jesus said to them, 'Very truly, I tell you, unless you eat the flesh of the Son of Man and drink his blood, you have no life in you. Those who eat my flesh and drink my blood have eternal life, and I will raise them up on the last day; for my flesh is true food and my blood is true drink. Those who eat my flesh and drink my blood abide in me, and I in them.'

It is crunch time. This passage comes when the disciples and the crowds following Jesus are finally starting to get the idea behind his teaching. Of course, they misunderstand some aspects and with other parts of it, they can't get their heads round the revolutionary nature of his message.

Here we can get to grips with the idea of living in Jesus. As we have seen, the good news is that he helps us. It's not a lonely commitment to an idea, but a joining in with a loving relationship. Now we can look more closely about how this can be sustained. We carry on in this relationship, this community of love, because Jesus feeds us. He provides sustenance with his own body, given for us. This is true food, which keeps us going through thick and thin.

That is why it's so important for us to worship, pray, read, meet with people who reflect God and share in services of Holy Communion. Communion is the love of God made real and physical—a gift we can see, touch and taste.

Joining in this feast makes us a part of our Lord's body; by eating the body of Christ, we become the body of Christ. As Augustine of Hippo said about taking and becoming this body, 'If you have received well, you are that which you have received', or, as we might even say, 'You are what you eat.'

Prayer

Grant us therefore, gracious Lord, so to eat the flesh of your dear Son Jesus Christ and to drink his blood, that our sinful bodies may be made clean by his body and our souls washed through his most precious blood, and that we may evermore dwell in him, and he in us.

Service of Holy Communion, *Common Worship*
RB

JOHN 6:64, 66–69 (NRSV, ABRIDGED)

'You are the Holy One of God'

'But among you there are some who do not believe.' For Jesus knew from the first who were the ones that did not believe… Because of this many of his disciples turned back and no longer went about with him. So Jesus asked the twelve, 'Do you also wish to go away?' Simon Peter answered him, 'Lord, to whom can we go? You have the words of eternal life. We have come to believe and know that you are the Holy One of God.'

Here, Jesus moves on to develop what the impact of his message can be. It's a message that demands a response, one way or the other, so it's only to be expected that some people turn away. The big problem is our indifference.

Jesus seems to have been particularly tough on people's lack of commitment—hardly the beard-and-sandals 'pale Galilean' of folklore. 'No one who puts a hand to the plough and looks back is fit for the kingdom of God', he advised potential followers (Luke 9:62). With all his love and forgiveness, he can deal with the questions, misunderstandings and enthusiasm of his disciples, but people's refusal to choose his path offers him nothing to go on.

In place of the 'whatever' shrug of indifference, Peter offers a thrilling restatement of what he has committed to: 'You have the words of eternal life'. Of course, Peter goes on to deny Jesus, but he is the supreme example of a disciple who shows that commitment means keeping going and trying again after failure. Harking back to the themes we considered yesterday—about joining in Jesus' body through Communion (the Eucharist)—Timothy Radcliffe OP writes, 'Jesus had promised that his Father and he would make their home with the apostles, and this is now achieved [at the end of the Gospels]. The Eucharist is our home, whatever we have done and been… God accepts our limited, fragile forgetful loves if that is all that we have to offer him now. If there is a place for Peter, who denied Jesus, then there are places for us all' (*Why Go to Church?*, Continuum, 2008).

Reflection

*Which of your fears are preventing you from being committed
to the Holy One of God?*

RB

The commissioning of the disciples

Now the eleven disciples went to Galilee, to the mountain to which Jesus had directed them. When they saw him, they worshipped him; but some doubted. And Jesus came and said to them, 'All authority in heaven and on earth has been given to me. Go therefore and make disciples of all nations, baptising them in the name of the Father and of the Son and of the Holy Spirit, and teaching them to obey everything that I have commanded you. And remember, I am with you always, to the end of the age.'

Sometimes, when we're bogged down in our fears and anxieties, we need the reassurance of these words: 'I am with you always.' As we saw on Tuesday, we need to remind ourselves of the way that the universe is formed by God and ruled by love. This isn't a sentimental gush of emotions, but the steadfast, long-term commitment of being joined in a community of sharing. We were created specifically for this. As we saw in Deuteronomy at the start of these readings, God has promised himself to us. It is only our selfishness that stops us keeping our promises to him.

That is why daily prayer is so vital. It's both a basic acknowledgment of our place in the universe and an exchange of love with our Creator. We have a fundamental need to offer ourselves up to our Father each day, to renew the bonds of affection and faith.

If this seems like a hard task, we could recall what we learned earlier about its being an act of love shared with God. It is God who prays within us: 'Likewise the Spirit helps us in our weakness; for we do not know how to pray as we ought, but that very Spirit intercedes with sighs too deep for words' (Romans 8:26).

The whole point is that we are becoming part of something bigger, joining with the God who loves us.

Reflection

We are sure He cares far more to make the best of us, and to do the most through us, than we have ever cared ourselves… That He really wants us, and needs us, is the wonder and strength of our life.

A.W. Robinson, *The Personal Life of the Clergy* (Longmans, Green, 1902)
RB

Profile of a prophet: Isaiah

One commentator on Isaiah wryly observes that in writing his book he felt like a very small mouse heroically nibbling at a very large piece of cheese! In condensing the prophet's message for these daily readings I have had a similar feeling. Where should I begin? What should I include? What should I leave out?

Eventually I decided to base the readings on the pivotal sixth chapter, which describes Isaiah's encounter with God in the temple. I use this as a basis for showing how profoundly that day shaped both the man and his message. In the pages that follow, we will look at his understanding of God, his awareness of sin and the provision of forgiveness, as well his sense of calling and willingness to persevere in the difficulty of his task. I am aware that some scholars identify two different authors for Isaiah, but my assumption throughout is that there is a unity to this book.

In some ways, Isaiah's experience is a pattern for what God longed to do for all his wayward children. He prophesied during a period of political turmoil, religious apostasy and moral decline. We could well describe his temple encounter as 'personal revival in the midst of spiritual decline.' Isaiah first experienced his own message, then courageously delivered the same message to the people of Judah and Jerusalem.

If stability was to return to the nation, it was to be because, once again, the people had placed their faith in God. If they were to be saved from disaster, they had to acknowledge their sin and reform their ways. If they were to experience blessing, they had to respond to God's word with obedience.

There is an obvious connection between the message of Isaiah and our times. His words have relevance for our nations, as well as our churches. Many of the political manoeuvrings he condemns we see repeated on today's international stage. The same societal sins are present and the same disregard for God. The answer remains the same, too. Change happens individually, person by person. What is needed is personal revival and that begins with you and me.

So, as we share these readings together, let's pray that we will encounter God afresh. We cannot change everything, but we can—with God's help—be changed ourselves.

Tony Horsfall

Isaiah the man

The vision concerning Judah and Jerusalem that Isaiah son of Amoz saw during the reigns of Uzziah, Jotham, Ahaz and Hezekiah, kings of Judah.

Isaiah is unusual in that he was not only a prophet but also a city dweller. His message was formed not through quiet contemplation in the countryside but in the hurly burly of the capital. He was a man of Jerusalem and loved the city, with all its spiritual significance, while not being blind to its faults. He seems to have come from a well-connected family, for he had access to kings and moved freely in royal circles. He has been described as a statesman and political activist, a man of the world, who was aware of what went on in the highest realms of politics, religion and commerce.

Not for Isaiah the quiet of the study, either. His faith was worked out in the noisy realities of family life. He was a married man, with two children, doing his best to balance his spiritual task with the job of raising a family. His wife was a prophetess, sharing his spiritual outlook on life, and his children were given names with prophetic significance. He lived in the real world, with his feet on the ground (8:1–4, 18).

Isaiah was one of the 'writing' prophets, making sure the word of God was preserved. He was an artist with words, poetic images and picturesque illustrations flowing from his pen. Profound spiritual truths are conveyed in the simplest of metaphors. He is the prophet most quoted in the New Testament, a favourite of Jesus and Paul.

His ministry spanned the reigns of four different kings, probably over a period of 50 years (roughly from 739 to 686BC). It was a time of high anxiety as the superpowers of Assyria and Babylon circled menacingly around Jerusalem and Judah. Closer to home, the northern tribes were separated and established with their own monarchy as the kingdom of Israel. Throughout it all, Isaiah's message remained loud and clear. Trust God, not human beings. Do what is right and just and things will work out, even now, but, if not, remember this: discipline will come. There will be judgment.

Prayer

Speak to me, Lord, where I am.

TH

An encounter with God

In the year that King Uzziah died, I saw the Lord seated on a throne, high and exalted, and the train of his robe filled the temple. Above him were seraphs, each with six wings: with two wings they covered their faces, with two they covered their feet, and with two they were flying. And they were calling to one another: 'Holy, holy, holy is the Lord Almighty; the whole earth is full of his glory.' At the sound of their voices the doorposts and thresholds shook and the temple was filled with smoke.

Uzziah died in 740BC. His death marked the end of a period of stability and prosperity, opening up a time of uncertainty. At such a moment Isaiah is reminded of who is actually in control. The earthly throne may be vacant, but God is still the one who rules.

Isaiah here paints a majestic picture of God in this moment of revelation. This is the sovereign Lord, the true and living God—not to be compared in any way with lifeless idols. His purposes will come to pass.

Moreover, he is a holy God, set apart from his creation. The seraphim ('burning ones') hasten to do his bidding, yet cover themselves humbly in his presence. These heavenly creatures, calling to one another, teach us the importance of service and the glory of worshipping God in humble adoration.

When God draws near, the very temple is shaken. Here is one whose presence not only comforts but also disturbs. Things we rely on for security are exposed for their unreliability, while he alone remains unshaken and unmoved. A hazy mist fills the building, indicative of the 'otherness' of God, reminding us of his mystery and hiddenness. We cannot always fathom God or even discern his ways. Sometimes we must remain silent in reverent submission.

Isaiah's understanding of God was enlarged by his vision and we must allow our concept of God to be expanded, too. So often we want a domesticated God whom we can control and manage, whose ways we can predict. We need to release him from our limited understanding, allowing him to be the majestic God who reigns on high.

Prayer

Reveal yourself to me, majestic Lord.

TH

ISAIAH 40:9–10 (NIV)

The Sovereign Lord

You who bring good tidings to Zion, go up on a high mountain. You who bring good tidings to Jerusalem, lift up your voice with a shout, lift it up, do not be afraid; say to the towns of Judah, 'Here is your God!' See, the Sovereign Lord comes with power, and his arm rules for him. See, his reward is with him, and his recompense accompanies him.

Isaiah has seen the Lord enthroned on high. The awareness that God is seated on the throne fills him with confidence, even in the midst of so much change and turmoil. Earthly events may take us by surprise and fill us with fear, but what holds us firm is the knowledge that God is in control. Here is good news indeed for a nervous population, and it needs to be announced with gusto.

The sovereignty of God is a truth that has anchored God's people down the centuries. It means the belief that his plans and purposes are being worked out despite the resistance of sinful human beings. It is the conviction that God is able to work even negative events into his overall purpose, and that, ultimately, his will shall triumph.

For Isaiah, earthly rulers operate only under the control of God. They may *think* they have power, but it is an illusion. God raises them up and he casts them down again (10:12). They may exalt themselves against God's people, but they can only do what he allows. Rezin and Pekah discovered this (7:1–9), as did Sennacherib (37:33–38). Even the mighty Persian emperor Cyrus was but an instrument in the hand of God (44:28; 45:1, 13).

At the same time, the plans of God are being irresistibly worked out. 'This is the plan determined for the whole world; this is the hand stretched out over all the nations,' says the prophet. 'For the Lord Almighty has purposed, and who can thwart him? His hand is stretched out, and who can turn it back?' (14:26–27).

Safety and stability, then, can only be found in God and Isaiah would have us lift up our gaze to see the Lord, high and lifted up, seated on the throne.

Prayer
Today, we dare to believe, Sovereign Lord, that you are in control.

TH

The Holy One of Israel

For this is what the high and lofty One says—he who lives forever, whose name is holy: 'I live in a high and holy place, but also with those who are contrite and lowly in spirit, to revive the spirit of the lowly and to revive the heart of the contrite... I have seen their ways, but I will heal them; I will guide them and restore comfort to them.

Isaiah is the prophet of holiness. Indeed, the word 'holy' is used in his book more than in the rest of the Old Testament combined. His favourite title for God appears to be 'the Holy One of Israel', used 25 times. Clearly, his vision of the thrice holy God had a profound impact on him.

Holiness speaks to us of moral purity and perfection and it is this that makes God so totally 'other' from sinful human beings. God is light—in him there is no darkness at all (1 John 1:5). He can only do that which is good, right and just. Holiness also speaks to us of separation. God is uniquely holy with no rivals; he is transcendent, above us, and beyond our reach.

All this might be discouraging were it not for the fact that God chooses to link himself to his people—he is the Holy One *of Israel* (my italics) and Isaiah is also fond of adding 'your Redeemer' (for example, 41:14; 43:14). The holy God makes it possible for sinful people to draw near to him. We shall explore the theme of forgiveness later, but we note here that God chooses to dwell with those who are contrite (sorry for their sin) and lowly of heart (humble in their attitude).

Indeed, we are reminded in these verses that God 'revives' such people—that is, puts his own life within them. This is the kind of revival that is always needed—the quickening of spiritual life, the renewal of faith, the restoration of passion and zeal. We should approach a holy God with reverence, but if we come with true humility we shall find that, rather than being kept at arm's length, we are drawn into a place of intimate fellowship.

Prayer

Breathe on me, breath of God, Fill me with life anew.

Edwin Hatch, 1878
TH

The incomparable God

To whom, then, will you compare God? What image will you compare him to? As for an idol, a metal worker casts it, and a goldsmith overlays it with gold and fashions silver chains for it. People too poor to present such an offering select wood that will not rot. They look for a skilled craftsman to set up an idol that will not topple. Do you not know? Have you not heard? Has it not been told you from the beginning? Have you not understood since the earth was founded? He sits enthroned above the circle of the earth, and its people are like grasshoppers.

Isaiah's encounter with the living God has shown him once and for all the futility of idolatry. No manmade god can in any way compare to the Sovereign Lord. He is the Creator, while they are objects fashioned by those who are themselves created beings.

Idolatry was a besetting sin among God's people. For some strange reason they always seemed to be attracted to the gods that other nations worshipped, finding themselves drawn to pagan practices and dark superstitions. At various times we see Isaiah exposing the futility of their ways. Idols cannot see, hear, speak or move. They are made of wood and overlaid with precious metals to give them worth, but in reality they are worthless, for they cannot help.

Perhaps we think we are too sophisticated to fall into the sin of idolatry, but how easy it is to worship manmade objects—a brand new car, a state-of-the-art TV, the latest mobile phone and so on. How easily, too, are our affections transferred to our hobbies, holidays, homes and gardens. Other people can become more important to us than God and our work (even our ministry) can take his place in our lives.

Even more subtly, we can create a god in our own image, fashioning our idea of God according to what *we* want him to be like, rather than the way he is presented to us in scripture. Our theology can become rigid, leaving no room for fresh revelations of God or new understandings of his ways. It may feel 'correct', but we may be worshipping an idol rather than the real thing.

Prayer

Deliver me from idolatry, Lord.

TH

The God of mystery

'For my thoughts are not your thoughts, neither are your ways my ways,' declares the Lord. 'As the heavens are higher than the earth, so are my ways higher than your ways and my thoughts than your thoughts.'

We are considering the picture of God that Isaiah paints for us following his vision in the temple. His vision is of a God who is majestic, rules over all the earth and is so much greater than any other so-called god. Why should we think that we could understand such a God with our finite minds? Yet we continue to try and squeeze him into our systems of thought.

Most of us want a God who is predictable—it is part of our need to be in control. Most of us also develop our own 'systematic theology'— that is, our understanding of how God is expected to work. When things work out as we expect and God stays within the little 'box' we have made for him, everything is fine. The problem comes when life throws up something unexpected, events that seem contrary to all we have previously understood. Then we have a problem understanding and encounter the mystery of God.

My early Christian life was full of certainty. I had been well trained in theology and thought I had answers to most of life's questions. As time has gone by, however, not only have some of my answers proved inadequate but also some situations have arisen for which I have no answer at all. I am left only with questions, a sense of my own inability to fathom everything, and the mystery of God. The temple has been shaken and there is smoke everywhere!

While the bedrock of my faith remains the same, there has certainly been development and change over time—more openness to others, and a greater ability to be at peace even when I do not know the answer—in other words, to embrace mystery. My God has not become smaller but larger, more in keeping with the majestic portrait of God penned for us by Isaiah. We may not always understand God, but we can always trust him. He isn't safe, but he is good.

Prayer

Lord, help us to live with questions, to be at home with mystery.

TH

Silenced by holiness

'Woe to me!' I cried. 'I am ruined! For I am a man of unclean lips, and I live among a people of unclean lips, and my eyes have seen the King, the Lord Almighty.' Then one of the seraphs flew to me with a live coal in his hand, which he had taken with tongs from the altar. With it he touched my mouth and said, 'See, this has touched your lips; your guilt is taken away and your sin atoned for.'

We return to the pivotal sixth chapter and Isaiah's experience in the temple. His encounter with God is utterly life changing, providing a new revelation of God and a new understanding of himself.

Confronted by the intensity of the holiness of God, the prophet is convicted of his sinfulness. We cannot imagine that he was unaware of his sins before, but now he is more intensely aware of himself as a sinner. 'Woe is me', he cries in anguish. The brightness of God shows up his true nature, just as sun shining on a window reveals the dirt. In the presence of God the prophet is 'ruined'—that is, exposed, shown up for what he is.

Then follows his confession. Any number of sins may have stained his conscience, but speech is highlighted. How significant this is for a man of words, a man whose calling is to communicate. There is probably no area of our lives where we sin more frequently than with our words—whether spoken, written or e-mailed. If you think you have no sin, consider your speech.

Finally comes his cleansing. God's purpose is not to demoralise him, but to build him up, and the answer to his sinfulness is provided from the altar, the place of sacrifice where atonement was made for sin. It speaks of Calvary, the once-for-all-time sacrifice made by Jesus on our behalf. Isaiah's lips are touched with a live coal, signifying the application of the atoning sacrifice to his life and bringing with it freedom from guilt and shame.

Isaiah's task will be to call Israel to repentance. He can do this with integrity because he has faced up to his own sinfulness.

Prayer

Lord, have mercy on me, a sinner.

TH

Isaiah 1:4, 7 (NIV)

A guilty people

Ah, sinful nation, a people loaded with guilt, a brood of evildoers, children given to corruption! They have forsaken the Lord; they have spurned the Holy One of Israel and turned their backs on him... Your country is desolate, your cities burned with fire; your fields are being stripped by foreigners right before you, laid waste as when overthrown by strangers.

Isaiah's calling is to confront the nation with its sinfulness. He does so not with the judgmental attitude of a moralist, but with the compassion of one who has had his own searching encounter with the thrice holy God.

The basic issue is not about breaking the law, but about a breakdown in relationship. Israel are the people of God, called to live in a covenant relationship with him, but they have broken that relationship. Notice the words that are used—'forsaken', 'spurned', 'turned their backs'. These are emotive terms, reflecting the gravity of their rejection of God and the pain it caused him. Turning away from God, they have given themselves to corruption in its many forms. Sinning has become their habitual pattern, a way of life, and they are weighed down with guilt, in God's sight if not in their own. What a sad state for a people destined to live in a holy relationship with a holy God.

Already the discipline of God is at work, not out of vengeance or bad temper, but in chastening love. The country has suffered the ravages of war and the blessings of God have been removed. This should be enough to awaken the people to their plight, but they are stubborn in their rebellion. God will allow their enemies to plunder them in the hope that it will bring them to their senses.

Too often we focus our attention on specific sins when all the time God is concerned about the bigger picture of our relationship with him. Each of us was made by God to know him and love and serve him. He wants us to live in relationship with him, experiencing his love and knowing his goodness. When we sin we don't just break his moral law, we break his heart.

Prayer

Forgive us, Lord, when we wander from you. Gently bring us back.

TH

When prayer doesn't work

When you spread out your hands in prayer, I will hide my eyes from you; even if you offer many prayers, I will not listen. Your hands are full of blood; wash and make yourselves clean. Take your evil deeds out of my sight! Stop doing wrong, learn to do right! Seek justice, encourage the oppressed. Defend the cause of the fatherless, plead the case of the widow.

The charges brought against the nation now become more specific, and two are highlighted in particular: hypocrisy and injustice. For Isaiah, true religion is expressed in the way we live, behave and care for the needy. As a covenant people, not only were they supposed to live in relationship with God but also with each other. This meant that they should have dealt justly with one another, expressing God's holiness in their righteous behaviour.

All around him Isaiah saw not justice but oppression. Exploitation and greed dominated life and the weak were not only marginalised but victimised, too. Orphans and widows in particular were abused and mistreated. Added to this, these same people appeared before God in worship, asking for his blessing in prayer. They could not see the inconsistency between how they are behaving on one hand and praying to a holy God on the other. They are going through the motions of prayer without realising that they are unclean before God. Their prayers would get no further than the ceiling, for God was no longer listening.

The remedy? A thoroughgoing repentance. First, they needed to make themselves clean by asking for God's forgiveness. Then, they had to stop their evil ways. Finally, it was imperative that they began to do what was right. Only then would God be able to hear their prayers.

For too long the Church has neglected its responsibility to care for people. Too often we have separated 'faith' from 'works', worshipping God but not getting involved in the needs of society around us. Sin is not just what we do; sometimes it is what we don't do. Our refusal to get our hands dirty in helping the needy is a sin of neglect. Each of us must ask, 'Lord, what would you have me to do?'

Prayer

Lord, let my faith live through my works.

TH

A reasonable offer

'Come now, let us reason together,' says the Lord. 'Though your sins are like scarlet, they shall be as white as snow; though they are red as crimson, they shall be like wool. If you are willing and obedient, you will eat the best from the land; but if you resist and rebel, you will be devoured by the sword.' For the mouth of the Lord has spoken.

Isaiah's own experience of cleansing had taught him that God is merciful and compassionate. As a prophet he was called to speak on God's behalf and, having exposed the sins of the nation, he now brings God's amazing offer of forgiveness.

God invites his people to consider their ways. Their sins cannot be hidden—they are red as scarlet, bright as crimson in the sight of God. Faced with the prophet's exposure of their deeds, they blush with shame for they have been caught red-handed, as it were. If the people have any conscience at all, they will acknowledge their guilt.

Alongside this comes the offer of forgiveness. If they admit their sin, God will cleanse them, washing away the stain of their evil deeds. Their consciences can be made as white as freshly fallen snow (free from guilt and condemnation); their hearts can become as white as wool (soft and gentle, responsive to God).

This was an amazing offer, but it was conditional. God wasn't going to force them into such a transaction; they had to be willing to respond and ready to obey in the future. If they did so, then the blessing of God would return to their lives and to the land. Should they resist and rebel, they would automatically bring themselves under the discipline of God, and it would increase in its severity.

Such an offer is one that any reasonable person would quickly respond to, but sin often prevents us from seeing reason. It deceives us and deludes us into thinking that we can sin with impunity, that our sin is too precious to give up. Forgiveness, cleansing, restoration—these are the gifts of God on offer today. Receive them with gladness.

Prayer
Lord, this is an offer I cannot refuse! Cleanse me, I pray.

TH

Forgiveness made possible

Surely he took up our infirmities and carried our sorrows, yet we considered him stricken by God, smitten by him, and afflicted. But he was pierced for our transgressions, he was crushed for our iniquities; the punishment that brought us peace was upon him, and by his wounds we are healed. We all, like sheep, have gone astray, each of us has turned to his own way; and the Lord has laid on him the iniquity of us all.

Isaiah has been called the 'evangelical' prophet because his message contains so much of what we call the 'gospel'. The apostle John notes that Isaiah 'saw Jesus' glory and spoke about him' (John 12:41). Here we have what many would consider an amazing example of the prophet's ability to see into the future, for this chapter contains a graphic and accurate description of the death of Jesus and its significance.

What stands out here is that his death would be a substitutionary one, on behalf of others. Once again we are faced with our sinfulness. We have transgressed God's laws; we have committed iniquities; we have gone astray in self-centred wandering. Yet, God has acted on our behalf, sending his Son to die in our place.

Something of the horror of the cross is glimpsed in such words as 'stricken', 'smitten', 'pierced' and 'crushed'. The just demands of the law are satisfied because Jesus died in our place, taking the punishment that our sins deserved. In merciful exchange, our iniquities were laid on him so that we might be pardoned. Two benefits flow from the cross. The first is peace, for we are now reconciled to God. The law's demands have been satisfied, the condemning voice of conscience silenced. The second is healing, for the broken relationship with God is restored. The self-inflicted wounds of sinful ways can begin to mend.

No truth inspires love and gratitude in our hearts more than this— that, while we were still sinners, Christ died for us (Romans 5:8). We stand beneath the cross of Jesus and allow its shadow to fall over us. Peace and healing flow towards us as we reach out in faith; worship and thanksgiving flow from us as we bow in silent adoration.

Prayer
Hallelujah, what a Saviour!

TH

The dilemma of heaven

Then I heard the voice of the Lord saying, 'Whom shall I send? And who will go for us?' And I said, 'Here am I. Send me!' He said, 'Go and tell this people: "Be ever hearing, but never understanding; be ever seeing, but never perceiving." Make the heart of this people calloused; make their ears dull and close their eyes. Otherwise they might see with their eyes, hear with their ears, understand with their hearts, and turn and be healed.'

We return once more to Isaiah's temple experience and the moment of his commissioning. He has been given a glimpse of God in his glory and of himself in his need. Now he is given a glimpse of what lies ahead of him.

The dilemma of heaven is a simple one. There are things that God wishes to accomplish on earth and he chooses to work through human beings to achieve his purposes. Someone is needed who will willingly embrace the heavenly vision. It seems a very risky strategy, given human nature, but it is the one God has chosen. He is able to draw a straight line even with a crooked stick!

Isaiah responds with whole-hearted obedience: 'Here I am. Send me!' Nothing delights the heart of God more than the absolute surrender indicated by these words, for they represent the highest expression of faith and love possible between God and his people. It is an unconditional offer, made in the belief that God's will is best (Romans 12:2) and his placement of us will be for our good.

That is not to say the task before us will be easy. Isaiah is informed that his message will fall on deaf ears. His oft-repeated call to repentance and offer of forgiveness will be rejected, serving to harden their hearts even more. Repeated resistance to the word of God eventually makes us insensitive and deaf to his voice.

Interestingly, this is one of the most quoted parts of Isaiah in the New Testament (Mark 4:12; John 12:39–41; Acts 28:26–27). Resistance to the word of God is an ever-present danger. God will never force his will on us, but waits for us to offer ourselves freely and willingly.

Prayer

Use me, Lord, use even me.

TH

ISAIAH 30:9–11 (NIV)

No more!

These are rebellious people, deceitful children, children unwilling to listen to the Lord's instruction. They say to the seers, 'See no more visions!' and to the prophets, 'Give us no more visions of what is right! Tell us pleasant things, prophesy illusions. Leave this way, get off this path, and stop confronting us with the Holy One of Israel!'

A feature of Isaiah's ministry, like that of most of the prophets, is that the message falls on deaf ears. As we have seen, he had been warned that this would be the case, but, because the danger of resisting the Holy Spirit remains a constant threat, we take time today to examine the issue more closely.

Prophets are uncomfortable people to have around. They disturb the status quo and refuse to settle for second best. They hold us to the highest standards and refuse to let us settle for mediocrity. They confront us with the truth, challenge our complacency and stand in the way of our sinful behaviour. They represent to us a holy God and will not compromise his standards. No wonder they are often vilified and attacked. It is easier to silence the messenger than receive a message that convicts.

People in Isaiah's day wanted prophets who would speak to them comfortable things, even if they were not true. It is the same today. It is a great temptation for all who communicate God's word to bring messages that people want to hear, preach a popular gospel that comforts but never offends. Yet, the God of the Bible is someone who disturbs as well as comforts, who shakes the foundations of the temple from time to time and whose presence can be disconcerting.

We must be willing to let down our defences and be open to what God has to say. We must have the courage to allow the Holy Spirit to speak to us and not be afraid if he convicts us of our sin or calls us to greater obedience. As obedient children, we should welcome the instruction of our loving heavenly Father. His only desire is to train us in his way and produce the fruits of righteousness in our lives.

Prayer

Speak, Lord, your servant is listening.

TH

A model servant

'Here is my servant, whom I uphold, my chosen one in whom
I delight; I will put my Spirit on him and he will bring justice to
the nations. He will not shout or cry out, or raise his voice in the
streets. A bruised reed he will not break, and a smouldering wick
he will not snuff out. In faithfulness he will bring forth justice; he
will not falter or be discouraged till he establishes justice on earth.
In his law the islands will put their hope.'

In contrast to the disobedience of most in Judah, Isaiah portrays an
unnamed servant who epitomises what it means to live in obedience to
God. Scholars debate the identity of this person. In some ways, Isaiah
himself fulfils this role, but, in other ways, his portrait describes the role
that God had intended for Israel. Only one person, however, completely
matches the picture—Jesus Christ.

Matthew has no doubt about the servant's identity: Isaiah is speaking prophetically of the coming Messiah and, therefore, of Jesus. His
ministry clearly fulfilled the description given by the prophet (Matthew
12:13–17). He is the one chosen by God, in whom God delights.

The servant's calling is to bring justice to the nations. We can think
of this justice in two ways. First, Jesus satisfied the just demands of the
law by his sacrificial death; and, second, he demonstrated the just rule
of God through his ministry of healing, deliverance and concern for the
poor. It was for this task that he was anointed by the Holy Spirit.

The servant's character is exemplary. There is no self-display, no
drawing attention to himself. He is not heavy-handed and doesn't lord it
over others, but deals with people in gentleness and grace. Nor does he
indulge in self-pity. Rather, he sees things through to the end, choosing
not to yield to discouragement or despair.

How beautifully Jesus embodies the role of the Servant. This is the
first of several 'servant songs' (49:1–6; 50:4–9; 52:13—53:12) and
each is fully lived out only by him. His example becomes a pattern for
our own life of service, for we are called to follow in his steps.

Prayer
Jesus, you are the Servant King and we follow you.

TH

How long, O Lord?

Then I said, 'For how long, O Lord?' And he answered: 'Until the cities lie ruined and without inhabitant, until the houses are left deserted and the fields ruined and ravaged, until the Lord has sent everyone far away and the land is utterly forsaken... But as the terebinth and oak leave stumps when they are cut down, so the holy seed will be the stump in the land.'

We turn for the last time to Isaiah 6 and hear the plaintive cry of the prophet when faced with the realisation that his ministry will be a difficult one. Perhaps we have all asked the question 'How long, O Lord?' at some point in our lives, so we can identify with Isaiah's anxious questioning.

God's answer can be summed up in one word: 'until'. Much had to happen before his mission would be completed and the burden of responsibility would not be lifted until these things were accomplished. Because of their persistent disobedience, the land would be ruined, their cities destroyed and the people carried away into exile.

The quality that Isaiah needed was faithfulness. His was not to be a 'successful' ministry (outwardly at least), but success was not his motivation anyway. His calling was to be faithful to the commission given him and to see it through to the end. This we know that Isaiah did, serving God faithfully for more than 50 years.

Yet his ministry was not without hope. There were a few people (a 'holy seed' or remnant) who remained faithful to God and heeded the prophet's message. Like a tree that has been cut down comes back to life, so the 'stump' of a purified Israel was to spring into life again. The destruction of the land and exile in a foreign country was not the end!

When we find ourselves asking 'How long, O Lord?', it is good for us to exercise faith and trust in God's timing and ordering of our lives. He will not leave us in any situation longer than necessary and, for every demand placed on us, he supplies the necessary grace. His timing is perfect and ours is in his hands.

Prayer
I wait for you, Lord.

TH

Bring them home

'Do not be afraid, for I am with you; I will bring your children from the east and gather you from the west. I will say to the north, "Give them up!" and to the south, "Do not hold them back." Bring my sons from afar and my daughters from the ends of the earth— everyone who is called by my name, whom I created for my glory, whom I formed and made.'

The seed of hope planted within Isaiah that day in the temple continued to grow within him. With the same prophetic insight that enabled him to foretell the birth, life and death of the Saviour, he was able to look forward to a day when God's people would return from exile and be settled again in their own land.

The second half of Isaiah (chapter 40 onwards) is filled with the confident expectation that the God who has disciplined his people through exile, will act again to restore grace and bring them safely home. Those events happened long after Isaiah had died, causing some to suggest that another person wrote this section (as mentioned in the Introduction). However, this is not a problem if we accept that prophetic ministry includes a predictive element.

Here we have the authoritative words of the Father commanding that his captive children be released. No power on earth (Babylonian or Persian) can withstand the liberating word of God as he comes to save his people. No matter how far they have wandered, even to the ends of the earth, he will bring them home.

The return from exile is one of the great redemptive acts of God, a parallel to the exodus, when Israel came into being. It reminds us that we have a God who never gives up on his erring children.

Isaiah's greatest gift was to place hope in the hearts of God's people. It is his abiding legacy to us as well: 'Strengthen the feeble hands, steady the knees that give way; say to those with fearful hearts, "Be strong, do not fear; your God will come… he will come and save you."' (35:3–4)

Prayer
God of hope, fill us with joy and peace as we trust you.

TH

Praying with Psalm 37

Why do bad things happen to good people? Why don't more bad things happen to bad people? These are the dilemmas at the heart of Psalm 37, part of a group of psalms (34—37) that have as their focus godliness and, by contrast, the fate of the wicked. It is generally acceptable to ask why the innocent suffer, but we are probably less comfortable dwelling on why wrongdoers don't get what they deserve when they deserve it. If we have been Christians for any length of time, we know that, like Jesus, we should love and pray for 'sinners'. The psalmists' talk of the 'righteous' may have uncomfortable overtones of self-righteousness to our ears.

While the modern tendency is to say that wrongdoing is due to individuals' being misunderstood or damaged in some way, the bracing attitude of the Bible is that we all have a choice—as we have had since the very beginning. The consequences of Adam and Eve's choice in Eden show that, given the ability to choose between good and evil, the human tendency is to go for evil in its various manifestations every time, from Cain murdering his brother in a jealous rage (why couldn't they have just had a fight and then made up?) to the marvel that is the worldwide web being used for the promotion of global terrorism, pornography and endless business scams.

One of the consolations promised to the godly in Psalm 37, and elsewhere, is that they will 'inherit the land', as first promised to Abraham (Genesis 12:1). This psalm is ascribed to David and so predates the catastrophe of the exile, whereby the nation lost the land, being led into captivity for repeatedly failing to keep the terms of God's covenant, choosing evil instead of good. Astonishingly, despite everything, he is willing to forgive them and eventually a remnant return home. The wicked and the righteous receive their just reward, but the outcome is always tempered by God's outrageous mercy.

The question still haunts us, though: why don't wrongdoers get what they deserve? Praying with this psalm lets us voice thoughts and emotions that we may consider too 'unChristian' to express except in the privacy of our hearts. Using the psalmist's words, we can bring ourselves, just as we are, into God's presence. We can tell him what we are thinking and feeling and then wait for his loving and healing response.

Naomi Starkey

Fret not

Do not fret because of those who are evil or be envious of those who do wrong; for like the grass they soon wither, like green plants they will soon die away. Trust in the Lord and do good; dwell in the land and enjoy safe pasture. Take delight in the Lord and he will give you the desires of your heart.

While we may not go around openly complaining about 'those who are evil', how many of us have not at some point looked with envy at somebody who has built a prosperous and successful life on the basis of values that we consider highly dubious? We may have worked hard over many years, been polite to our supervisors, reliable at all times—and then we see a colleague promoted over our heads whom we know to be disloyal and unkind, yet, apparently, their 'face fits', which is considered more important. We may go home and complain angrily to anybody who'll listen, 'It's not fair! Let's all trample on everybody else, because that's clearly the way to get on!'

The psalmist, though, tells us not to 'fret' (a wonderful word) because 'those who do wrong' are as transient as grass. 'That's all very well', we may respond, 'but they still seem to be flourishing nicely. Exactly when will they start withering?' This is the challenge: we have to trust that God's way is the best way, even if we feel as if we are waiting endlessly for the benefits to come through.

What we are called to do is 'dwell in the land' where we can enjoy 'safe pasture'. Ours is to be long-term, rooted and sustainable growth, a bit like the difference between flowers that pop up in the local park and look lovely for a week or two and trees that mature over decades until they are big enough to endure conditions that would wipe out those showy, but transient blooms. The final verse here brings a wonderful promise: if we 'delight' (the Hebrew word implies intense pleasure, not just a hesitant 'Er, that's nice' response) in the Lord, he will give us what we most long for.

Reflection

What is your heart's desire? Bring it to God and await his response.

NS

I'm telling you again—fret not

Commit your way to the Lord; trust in him and he will do this: he will make your righteous reward shine like the dawn, your vindication like the noonday sun. Be still before the Lord and wait patiently for him; do not fret when people succeed in their ways, when they carry out their wicked schemes. Refrain from anger and turn from wrath; do not fret—it leads only to evil. For those who are evil will be destroyed, but those who hope in the Lord will inherit the land. A little while, and the wicked will be no more; though you look for them, they will not be found. But the meek will inherit the land and enjoy peace and prosperity.

In case we hadn't got the message, the psalmist tells us again (and again): don't fret. Instead of agonising about our circumstances, wringing our hands over whether we have made the right decisions or not and even mentally stamping our feet and shouting for God to *do* something, we are to be patient and 'still before the Lord'.

In Psalm 46:10 we find a better-known verse, one that has inspired many songs of worship: 'Be still, and know that I am God'. In Psalm 37, though, the context is less praise to the Lord, more robust advice for his people. If we decide that patience is a second-best approach to life, we should heed the warning that anger and impatience can actually lead to 'evil'. Frustration is an ugly, fast-growing weed (I'm thinking Japanese knotweed) that, if we are not careful, can grow until it smothers any trace of peace and joy.

As well as 'inheriting the land' (a promise resonating with Jesus' 'Blessed are the meek, for they will inherit the earth', Matthew 5:5), those who wait patiently are also promised 'peace and prosperity'. Such words may not particularly stir our hearts, but we should remember that, wherever we are (and there are *New Daylight* readers across the globe), we are only a plane-ride away from places where 'peace and prosperity' remain a distant dream. This is a promise to treasure.

Prayer

Lord God, we release into your loving hands our frustration and impatience; grant us a measure of your infinite patience.

NS

The baddies' come-uppance

The wicked plot against the righteous and gnash their teeth at them; but the Lord laughs at the wicked, for he knows their day is coming. The wicked draw the sword and bend the bow to bring down the poor and needy, to slay those whose ways are upright. But their swords will pierce their own hearts, and their bows will be broken. Better the little that the righteous have than the wealth of many wicked; for the power of the wicked will be broken, but the Lord upholds the righteous.

The picture painted in these verses is a classic cartoon moment: the bad guy picks up an enormous hammer to crush the little guy and manages to hit himself on the head. He plants one of those fizzing fuse bombs, which explodes and leaves him blinking in a smear of soot. Watching events unfold is the Lord, laughing at the stupidity of those who think that they can destroy those whom he holds close to his heart.

In parts of scripture we find the assurance that the righteous will be blessed with material prosperity, so it is very interesting to find righteousness equated with poverty here. That is why a 'proof-texting' approach to the Bible can lead to such a plethora of dodgy ideas. What one passage says has to be held in tension with the different perspectives found elsewhere. This psalm describes a context in which being good has to be its own reward, at least for now. Everybody else is 'on the make' and doing extremely well—for now. That, though, is not how the story will end.

Whereas yesterday's reading warned of the need for patience, today's is a call to contentment. We must be content with what we have, even if it is less than we feel we deserve, because we have a wider perspective. As Jesus pointed out (Matthew 6:19–24), we can store 'treasure in heaven', with the promise, a few verses later (v. 33), that, if we seek to live by the values of God's kingdom, we will find that our earthly needs (remembering that they are not the same as wants) are supplied as well.

Prayer

Lord God, we release into your loving hands our neediness; grant us your peace that passes understanding.

NS

Vanishing in a puff of smoke

The blameless spend their days under the Lord's care, and their inheritance will endure for ever. In times of disaster they will not wither; in days of famine they will enjoy plenty. But the wicked will perish: though the Lord's enemies are like the flowers of the field, they will be consumed, they will go up in smoke. The wicked borrow and do not repay, but the righteous give generously; those the Lord blesses will inherit the land, but those he curses will be destroyed.

The promised blessings here sound reckless in their generosity—plenty in times of famine? How could this happen in an era before NGOs, charity media campaigns and government aid programmes? Even a cursory reading of Leviticus and Deuteronomy, though, confirms that God's laws were designed to create a community where all had enough and the poor and needy were cared for, even when times were hard. The actions of Joseph in Egypt (Genesis 41:41–57) also show that food aid programmes are no modern invention.

The blessings of God's kingdom are released when the values of his kingdom permeate a community and the individuals within it. In a society characterised by mistrust and corruption, nobody sees the point of investing in the 'common life'—and that is why God's people are called to be 'salt and light' (another link to the Sermon on the Mount). It is easy to assume that any kind of God-given 'call' must be to full-time church ministry or being a mission worker somewhere very hot and daunting, but is it not also possible that we may be called to work for God, embodying the values of God, in business, government or the public sector?

We also find here the troubling idea of the Lord's 'curse', the wicked 'going up in smoke'. It is troubling to think of God being anything other than love, yet within scripture we find promises of mercy and forgiveness as well as stern warnings about the consequences of sinful, rebellious behaviour. If we choose to go our own way, we will be allowed to do so, though the outcomes will be very different.

Prayer and reflection

Pray for your local government councillors—and consider whether God might be calling you or somebody you know to serve him in that context.

NS

Reciprocal generosity

The Lord makes firm the steps of those who delight in him; though they stumble, they will not fall, for the Lord upholds them with his hand. I was young and now I am old, yet I have never seen the righteous forsaken or their children begging bread. They are always generous and lend freely; their children will be a blessing.

We only have to browse Internet news sites or newspapers to be taken aback by the forthright confidence expressed in these verses. It is all too easy to find examples of countries where devout Christians and their families are starving and suffering. This psalm is identified as being 'of David', so are we supposed to take this as literally suggesting that no good people ever went hungry in his lifetime in ancient Israel—or is this poetic licence? I think the key to the point being made lies in the final sentence: the righteous are not forsaken—and they are also characterised by being 'always generous'.

Let me explain: as we reflected yesterday, when a society becomes characterised by godly virtues such as kindness, patience, love and generosity, then all benefit, whatever their material status. In this, we can detect a foreshadowing of Jesus' words, 'Ask and it will be given to you; seek and you will find; knock and the door will be opened to you' (Matthew 7:7). We tend to read this verse from the Sermon on the Mount as relating to persistence in prayer, but imagine the impact if such a pattern of mutual giving and receiving characterised the everyday life of a community or even a whole country!

I read an analysis of American concerns about government healthcare reforms, which argued that resistance to national initiatives sprang in part from a desire to return to the days when charitable works arose naturally from the neighbourly impulses of small-town life, as opposed to 'welfare' imposed by an impersonal system of taxation and legal decree. The extent to which that idyllic 'old-time' scenario was ever realised is debatable, but the principle involved remains a challenging one.

Reflection
Supporting fair trade initiatives is an excellent way to play a part in the building of global systems that provide mutual benefit. Is yours a fair trade church?

NS

People of the land

Turn from evil and do good; then you will dwell in the land for ever. For the Lord loves the just and will not forsake his faithful ones. Wrongdoers will be completely destroyed; the offspring of the wicked will perish. The righteous will inherit the land and dwell in it for ever. The mouths of the righteous utter wisdom, and their tongues speak what is just. The law of their God is in their hearts; their feet do not slip. The wicked lie in wait for the righteous, seeking their very lives; but the Lord will not leave them in their power or let them be condemned when brought to trial.

We now reflect a bit further on the central promise of this psalm, that the righteous will 'inherit the land'. The land means the Promised Land, the land of Israel, the precise borders of which were not made entirely clear, although a commonly used term was 'from Dan to Beersheba' (1 Samuel 3:20; 1 Kings 4:25; 2 Chronicles 30:5). 'The Land', *Haaretz* in Hebrew, is today the name of Israel's oldest daily newspaper (founded in 1918 while the British ruled what was then Palestine).

To us, the idea of 'inheriting the land' may have overtones of being 'landed gentry'. If we own land, we have power over it and even over any people who may live on it, although that power is limited by law. I recall, not so many years ago, speaking to a woman who still remembered her father's fear of losing his tied cottage if the lord of the manor did not see him in church on Sundays.

All talk of 'the land' in the Old Testament, though, was balanced by the astonishing terms of the Year of Jubilee (Leviticus 25:8–55). Every 50 years, all land was to be returned to its original owners, so nobody amassed property and passed it down through their family forever. Thus, the righteous will inherit the land, but remain tenants of the Lord, who, if they are faithful to his covenant with them, will be the most benevolent of landlords.

Reflection

'If you follow my decrees... I will walk among you and be your God, and you will be my people' (Leviticus 26:12).

NS

The Lord our stronghold

Hope in the Lord and keep his way. He will exalt you to inherit the land; when the wicked are destroyed, you will see it. I have seen the wicked and ruthless flourishing like a luxuriant native tree, but they soon passed away and were no more; though I looked for them, they could not be found. Consider the blameless, observe the upright; a future awaits those who seek peace. But all sinners will be destroyed; there will be no future for the wicked. The salvation of the righteous comes from the Lord; he is their stronghold in times of trouble; the Lord helps them and delivers them; he delivers them from the wicked and saves them, because they take refuge in him.

It is interesting to see how the imagery develops in this psalm. In the opening verses, the wicked are like grass and green plants, lush but transient. Later on, they are compared to meadow flowers but now they are said to flourish 'like a luxuriant native tree'. Hang on, isn't such strength and vigour supposed to be the preserve of God's favoured ones, who (according to Isaiah 61:3) 'will be called mighty oaks, a planting of the Lord for the display of his splendour'? The ruthless people here are not only still growing; they now look like a deeply rooted and traditional part of the landscape, protected by tree preservation orders.

Leaping to the very end of the Bible, we find the evil forces opposing God portrayed in terrifying imagery of dragons, giant insects, horned sea-monsters and an army so vast that they are like the sand on the seashore (Revelation 20:8). The book of Revelation does not spare us the horror—but neither does it diminish the scale of the victory, already won, of light over darkness.

However unchecked and pervasive the might of the wicked, however apparently hopeless the plight of the righteous, there is always the firm hope of deliverance. For the psalmist, that deliverance comes through the Lord, our 'stronghold in times of trouble'; for the writer of Revelation, there is the assurance of the almighty power on the throne of heaven and the risen Lamb of God.

Prayer

Almighty Father, you are our strong tower. We shelter in you and know that in you we can hope for deliverance.

NS

Bible places: Bethlehem and Nazareth

If you go to either Bethlehem or Nazareth today, you will find a bustling town, with a population in the tens of thousands and a steady torrent of visitors coming to see the biblical sites. For these are the towns of Jesus' childhood. Bethlehem, say the Gospels, was the place of his birth and Nazareth of his upbringing. Yet, in Jesus' day, they were much smaller places, of only a few hundred people: we would call them villages rather than towns.

Bethlehem stands among the Judean hills, south of Jerusalem. Some of the surrounding land is good farmland, with orchards of olive trees and terraced slopes where crops grow. Perhaps it was on slopes like these that Ruth gleaned for grain, in the fields of Boaz. East of the town, towards the desert, the land is too dry to cultivate. Shepherds find just enough grass for their sheep and goats, just as David did when he watched his flocks 3000 years ago.

Nazareth is much further north, not far from Lake Galilee. It stands on a ridge, looking across the fertile Plain of Jezreel. To the north you can see Sepphoris, once the chief town of Galilee. Indeed Sepphoris was rebuilt, in some style and at great expense, while Jesus was growing up. Might he have served his apprenticeship there, working with Joseph on the building sites of the new city? We don't know; Sepphoris is not mentioned in the Bible.

Nazareth, too, does not appear in the Old Testament; only in the New. It may have been a newish settlement then, formed when people from around Jerusalem migrated northwards, about 100BC. It was in this community, away from the main centres of rule and riches, that Jesus shared a family home, grew to his adult years and first learned to work in wood. Here he worshipped, and from here he went out to be baptised and tell of God's kingdom.

Bethlehem is mentioned often in the Bible. We shall start with the story of two faithful women in the Book of Ruth. David comes next, then the prophet Micah points forwards, in hope and anticipation, to a future king—to Jesus, according to Matthew's Gospel. We read of Jesus' birth and of the Holy Family travelling down to Egypt and on to Nazareth. Our final readings show the adult Jesus calling disciples and coming home to preach in the local synagogue.

John Proctor

RUTH 1:15–19A (NRSV, ABRIDGED)

Sorrow and love

So [Naomi] said, 'See, your sister-in-law has gone back to her people and her gods; return after your sister-in-law.' But Ruth said, 'Do not press me to leave you or to turn back from following you! Where you go, I will go; where you lodge, I will lodge; your people shall be my people, and your God my God. Where you die, I will die—there will I be buried...' When Naomi saw that she was determined to go with her, she said no more to her. So the two of them went on until they came to Bethlehem.

We join this story after a cascade of misfortunes. Naomi and her family had left Bethlehem in a time of famine for the land of Moab on the far side of Jordan (v. 1). There, Naomi's husband and two sons died, leaving three widows leaning on each other for support (vv. 3–5). Orpah and Ruth belonged to Moab. Naomi hankered for Bethlehem, where there was food to be had now and the familiar landmarks of her memories. Naomi understood when Orpah decided to stay in Moab—it was Orpah's homeland, after all—but Ruth joined Naomi on the road.

What drew Ruth to Naomi and to Bethlehem? Practical reasons, perhaps, but her personal attachment to Naomi was surely a big factor. When life's closest bonds are broken, people matter more than places; we need someone, not simply somewhere. There seems to be a spiritual concern, too. Had Naomi's steadiness in sorrow shown Ruth something of her faith and of the face of her God? Had Ruth started to trust this God, too?

So it was that the two of them travelled on. On a clear day, you can see to Bethlehem from Moab, yet there is a deep valley between them, as well as the Dead Sea and desert. Their journey required a deliberate going down and a hard climb up to the new life ahead. Naomi was going home, but for Ruth it was a foreign land. What would she find? What would become of her there?

Reflection and prayer

Remember someone you know who has trusted God in the midst of sorrow and uncertainty. Give thanks for them. Pray for anyone you know who is coping with loss today or trying to settle somewhere new.

JP

God of the generations

So Boaz took Ruth and she became his wife. When they came together, the Lord made her conceive, and she bore a son. Then the women said to Naomi, 'Blessed be the Lord, who has not left you this day without next-of-kin; and may his name be renowned in Israel! He shall be to you a restorer of life and a nourisher of your old age; for your daughter-in-law who loves you, who is more to you than seven sons, has borne him.' Then Naomi took the child and laid him in her bosom… They named him Obed; he became the father of Jesse, the father of David.

The book of Ruth ends well. Naomi had been away a long time, but she still had title to land in Bethlehem. There was an extended family, too, who had some duty to help her and continue, if possible, her family line. So Boaz bought the land and married Ruth. The Bible tells of it as not merely a legal arrangement but also a marriage of devotion and delight.

A son was born. Naomi would care for him through childhood, rejoice as he grew to maturity and depend on him as she got old. Bethlehem had restored the hopes and future that she surely thought had been buried in Moab. Her journey had brought her home to welcome and joy. Boaz, too, had an heir for his considerable wealth and resources. Also, Ruth had a place in the community—a home, a role, a family circle, acceptance and belonging.

There we might be tempted to leave them, but the book of Ruth is surely more than this. It leaves a thread trailing into the future: Obed, Jesse, David. Ruth was the great-grandmother of Israel's greatest king; she was a link in the royal line.

Bethlehem became a refuge for Ruth and there her faithful love shaped Israel's future. She was part of David's heritage and part, too, of Jesus' family line, for Ruth is one of four Gentile women in Jesus' genealogy (Matthew 1:5). Israel's Christ reflects and draws into himself the love and longing of the nations.

Prayer
*Pray for refugees, that they may find ways to give love and service
in the places to which they come.*

JP

Not the obvious people

The Lord said to Samuel, '… Fill your horn with oil and set out; I will send you to Jesse the Bethlehemite, for I have provided for myself a king among his sons.'… When [the sons] came, he looked on Eliab and thought, 'Surely the Lord's anointed is now before the Lord.' But the Lord said to Samuel. 'Do not look on his appearance… for the Lord does not see as mortals see; they look on the outward appearance, but the Lord looks on the heart.'… And [Jesse] said, 'There remains yet the youngest, but he is keeping the sheep.'… The Lord said, 'Rise and anoint him; for this is the one.' Then Samuel took the horn of oil, and anointed him in the presence of his brothers; and the spirit of the Lord came mightily upon David from that day forward.

Anointing was the point and purpose of Samuel's errand, and it was a turning point in David's life. The Hebrew word for anointed is 'messiah', meaning a person marked out by God for a major task or responsibility. Oil is almost invisible, yet, under the light of heaven, anointing shines clear and bright. Like a security mark on a piece of valuable property, it is a sign of ownership and belonging.

This is a story about divine choice. God does not always use the obvious people, nor the most experienced. Samuel had to listen carefully to God to make sure that he picked the right son. David's eldest brother looked impressive, but God sees potential and shapes personalities in ways we could never guess.

David did not speak or act at this stage, yet he was marked out for a new career. The Spirit started to blow through his life, to equip him for the stresses and service ahead. Bethlehem, too, was a community changed. It would become a royal town, the new king's home. It was as if the oil poured on to David ran down into the soil to anoint the very ground. Bethlehem was a place with potential. It was not the most obvious setting for grandeur, yet it had been chosen by God.

Prayer

God of strange calls and sure choices, help me to honour the gifts you put into other people and the duties you ask of me.

JP

2 SAMUEL 23:13–17 (NRSV, ABRIDGED)

Water of life

Towards the beginning of harvest… David was then in the stronghold; and the garrison of the Philistines was then at Bethlehem.
David said longingly, 'O that someone would give me water to drink
from the well of Bethlehem that is by the gate!' Then the three
warriors broke through the camp of the Philistines, drew water
from the well of Bethlehem that was by the gate, and brought it
to David. But he would not drink of it; he poured it out to the Lord,
for he said, 'The Lord forbid that I should do this. Can I drink the
blood of the men who went at the risk of their lives?'

Today's reading recalls the period when David was an outlaw, hunted
by King Saul and hiding in the wilderness. The Philistines were Israel's
foes for generations. Their home was the coastal plain of the Holy Land,
going north from the town of Gaza, but here we see them reaching far
inland. When they camped at Bethlehem, the town's fields and the
year's food were at their mercy.

David remembered home and happier days. He was on the run,
and his life was in peril. A taste of well water would be a moment of
normality. 'If only,' he sighed, and three of his best warriors took it as
a challenge. Whether by speed or by stealth, they reached the well and
brought back a jar of water to their leader.

For David, their gift was sacred. Not because it was from Bethlehem,
but because good men had risked their lives to fetch it. The jar was full,
not merely with water, nor the taste of home, but with loyalty and courage. It was too solemn an offering to swallow; it had to be sacrificed, in
thanksgiving to God.

Reflection

*Even now, the spot mentioned in the passage is still pointed out to
visitors—three cisterns on the eastern edge of Bethlehem, traditionally
called 'David's wells'. The text reaches into the present in other ways, too.
It can be used on Remembrance Day, to recall the risks of war and the
respect due to those who meet them. It speaks about qualities of leadership,
humility and honour. It reminds us, too, that water is a costly resource
in many parts of the world.*

JP

Prince and protector

But you, O Bethlehem of Ephrathah, who are one of the little clans of Judah, from you shall come forth for me one who is to rule in Israel, whose origin is from of old, from ancient days... And he shall stand and feed his flock in the strength of the Lord, in the majesty of the name of the Lord his God. And they shall live secure, for now he shall be great to the ends of the earth; and he shall be the one of peace.

Micah lived nearly 300 years after David, in troubled times. Foreign armies stalked through God's land. Spirits were low and hope in short supply. Yet, his words reached beyond the troubles, to a future that would be secure under the strong hand of God. A leader would rise up, someone to give care and confidence, and point people to the kingly rule of God. From little Bethlehem, David's town, a king would come. Like David, the new leader would be a shepherd king, for the arts of shepherding are also the qualities of kingship: vigilance, courage, concern for individuals, constant care. Great leaders need to be protective, watchful and unselfish.

Micah spoke of a king who would carry the presence and power of God. There would be a touch of eternity about him. He would communicate a sense of God's ancient and enduring love and his fame would spread to the nations. The whole world would come to know of his greatness.

Who could such a leader be? The New Testament has an answer. Matthew's Gospel (2:6) takes up this text from Micah, as it tells of wise men searching for a newborn king in Israel. The text led them on from Jerusalem to Bethlehem and Jesus. Only he really fulfils Micah's hopes: the truly good shepherd; the leader who embodies the kingdom of God; the ruler whose roots were before time and outside history; the prince of peace whom the world would honour. In Jesus' coming, Micah's word would reach across the centuries and Bethlehem would raise up a new shepherd king.

Prayer
Remember places on earth where hope is hard to find: pray for good leaders, people of wise vision and godly faith.

JP

Child at the centre

In the time of King Herod, after Jesus was born in Bethlehem of Judea, wise men from the East came to Jerusalem, asking, 'Where is the child who has been born king of the Jews? For we observed his star at its rising, and have come to pay him homage.'... When they had heard the king, they set out; and there, ahead of them, went the star that they had seen at its rising, until it stopped over the place where the child was... On entering the house, they saw the child with Mary his mother; and they knelt down and paid him homage. Then, opening their treasure-chests, they offered him gifts of gold, frankincense, and myrrh.

This chapter of Matthew quotes directly from Micah's prophecy. The words we read yesterday appear at verse 6 and the verses in today's passage help to fill out what Matthew meant by using it. 'He shall be great to the ends of the earth', said Micah, and the wise men give the Gospel a view beyond Israel, to distant lands. With their longing, their learning and their love, they travelled to worship. With their gifts they brought the wealth of far countries. As they come to Bethlehem, we see Jesus as a magnet who will gather the peoples of the earth.

'His origin is of old, from ancient days', said Micah, and now the light of the Bethlehem star was shining on Jesus, with the praise of God's whole creation. His birth gladdened the universe. New glory in heaven welcomed the Messiah's coming to earth. He bore in himself the nature and goodness of God and carried into time the love of eternity.

In Jesus' coming, Bethlehem found its full glory. He was the fulfilment, beside whom David had been only a foreshadowing of the coming King. In Jesus' strange and humble birth, this tucked-away little town took its place at the centre of history. Here the Word, who had become flesh, first shared the air and light in which we live. In Jesus, Micah's words found a home and, in Jesus, so may we.

Prayer

Lord Jesus Christ, as wise men brought you gifts from far, may your good news be welcomed today, in fresh places and among faithful people.

JP

Tale of two cities

In those days a decree went out from Emperor Augustus that all the world should be registered. This was the first registration and was taken while Quirinius was governor of Syria. All went to their own towns to be registered. Joseph also went from the town of Nazareth in Galilee to Judea, to the city of David called Bethlehem, because he was descended from the house and family of David. He went to be registered with Mary, to whom he was engaged and who was expecting a child.

Matthew tells of Jesus' birth against the background of the Old Testament. His view into the wider world comes through mysterious eastern travellers and a guiding star. Luke's Gospel, by contrast, is more keenly aware of the Roman Empire, of the Roman network of law, roads and taxation that reached across the ancient world.

A Roman census was a cumbersome affair. The main aim was to tax people properly, to ensure that landowners in particular were paying their dues to the empire. So Joseph's journey made sense, if he had property in Bethlehem. As the owner, he would have needed to claim it and be assessed. Property might have come his way through family roots in the area, as 'he was descended from the house of David'.

Two kingdoms sit side by side in Luke's account—Rome and Bethlehem; the great city and the 'little town'. Here, Roman Caesar met the line of David. One held power and the other carried the promise of God. Augustus gathered and grasped; in Bethlehem, God gave a child who would himself send out a decree of good news and embrace the world.

In today's reading we hear Nazareth mentioned for the first time. Joseph came from there and, in a couple of days, we shall follow Joseph and Mary back to the north. For the moment, let us rejoice that, with God, small may indeed be beautiful. God often works in quiet ways, away from the centres of human power. Bethlehem had a gift to share with the world, greater than all the splendours of empire.

Prayer

Generous God, help me to see where you are at work in our world and rejoice in the strength and sureness of your grace.

JP

Tyranny and tears

Now after they had left, an angel of the Lord appeared to Joseph in a dream and said, 'Get up, take the child and his mother, and flee to Egypt, and remain there until I tell you; for Herod is about to search for the child, to destroy him.'... When Herod saw that he had been tricked by the wise men, he was infuriated, and he sent and killed all the children in and around Bethlehem who were two years old or under, according to the time that he had learned from the wise men.

Herod the Great was a ruthless king. The Roman Empire let him rule for a long time and he left a trail of bloodshed across his land, yet, as he grew older, he became insecure and saw threats on every side, even executing three of his sons because he thought they were too keen to succeed him. Amid the terrors of Herod's reign, the massacre of the innocents at Bethlehem is credible indeed.

Herod casts a grim shadow over the Christmas cradle. He looms above the manger as a sign of the evil in the world that Jesus knew. Crosses were common in the land where he was crucified. Children were slaughtered in the town of his birth.

The point of today's reading is surely not that the Christ escaped while others suffered and died. In this episode, Jesus was indeed preserved, but eventually his enemies caught up with him. He faced his own brutal death head-on, with the clear eyes of an adult and the knowledge, pain and fear that go with that clear sight. God's Messiah did not escape the hurts of earth. He entered into them and bore them. Here, at the very start of Matthew's Gospel, is a glimpse of the cross ahead.

Near Bethlehem today, you can still see the remains of a hilltop castle called Herodion. Herod built it as a stronghold and a sign of his power and control. His tomb has recently been discovered there. Tyrants die, but Christ is risen.

Prayer

Children suffer in many lands, through war, hunger, disease, violence, abuse. Pray for people who work to protect them—relief agencies, health-workers, police, social workers, carers.

JP

Safe home

When Herod died, an angel of the Lord suddenly appeared in a dream to Joseph in Egypt and said, 'Get up, take the child and his mother, and go to the land of Israel, for those who were seeking the child's life are dead.' Then Joseph got up, took the child and his mother, and went to the land of Israel. But when he heard that Archelaus was ruling over Judea in place of his father Herod, he was afraid to go there. And after being warned in a dream, he went away to the district of Galilee. There he made his home in a town called Nazareth, so that what had been spoken through the prophets might be fulfilled, 'He will be called a Nazorean.'

Herod was dead and the way clear for the holy family to return home. Joseph's dreams recall the experience of another Joseph (Genesis 37—41). He too was a dreamer and a protector of God's people in Egypt. Jesus, like Israel of old, could not stay in Egypt but had to return to grow up in his own land.

The family was careful about where it settled. Herod's kingdom had been divided among his three surviving sons. Archelaus was the worst of these. After a savage and unsatisfactory reign, Rome kicked him out and took direct control of his lands, but at that time he was still in power, so Bethlehem was full of dangers and Joseph and Mary could not go there. They made their way back to Nazareth in the north, away from the hub of national life. That was a safer place to reconnect with their own people, reopen the carpentry shop and embark on the long and loving task of raising a family.

For Matthew, the name Nazareth opened up an Old Testament connection (v. 23), but we cannot now be sure which prophet he was quoting. The most likely text is Isaiah 11:1, which promises a leader who is a 'branch' from David's family tree. The Hebrew word for 'branch' is nezer and Matthew spotted the resonance between that word and Nazareth. Jesus the Nazareth-man would also be a nezer-man, the promised royal leader from the line of David.

Prayer

Pray for families who cannot find a safe and settled home.

JP

Postcode prejudice

The next day Jesus decided to go to Galilee. He found Philip and said to him, 'Follow me.' Now Philip was from Bethsaida, the city of Andrew and Peter. Philip found Nathanael and said to him, 'We have found him about whom Moses in the law and also the prophets wrote, Jesus son of Joseph from Nazareth.' Nathanael said to him, 'Can anything good come out of Nazareth?' Philip said to him, 'Come and see.' When Jesus saw Nathanael coming toward him, he said of him, 'Here is truly an Israelite in whom there is no deceit!'

Never judge a person by where they live, the school they attended, the land they grew up in or the nation they belong to. Surroundings may nourish character, but they don't fix it. If we wrap other people in our prejudice, we may be surprised when we discover what they're really like. This surely happened for Nathanael.

After his baptism, Jesus set about recruiting followers to join his mission. Like many people today, he had to face prejudice—from Nathanael, for one. Nathanael belonged to Cana, quite near Nazareth (John 21:2) and surely knew how modest a place Nazareth was. There were many little towns in Galilee, but Nazareth was just a village. Who would follow a Nazarene?

'Come and see', said Philip (v. 46), yet it was Jesus who 'saw Nathanael' (v. 47). The encounter did not happen quite as Nathanael expected. Before he had any opportunity to size Jesus up, Jesus had worked him out as being 'an Israelite in whom there is no deceit'. Jesus was right. Nathanael was a straightforward character. He used words in direct ways, with no subtlety or subterfuge. Jesus understood him and took him on as a disciple, to travel with him and support his ministry.

In some ways Nathanael's encounter with Jesus is a pattern for ours. When we come near to Jesus, he always knows us better than we know him. If we bring our prejudices, he can face them and change us. If we meet him directly and honestly, we may well find that he trusts us much more fully than we expected.

Prayer

Lord Jesus Christ, thank you that you love the people I find it hard to love.

JP

Departure board

When [Jesus] came to Nazareth, where he had been brought up, he went to the synagogue on the sabbath day, as was his custom. He stood up to read, and the scroll of the prophet Isaiah was given to him. He unrolled the scroll and found the place where it was written: 'The Spirit of the Lord is upon me, because he has anointed me to bring good news to the poor. He has sent me to proclaim release to the captives and recovery of sight to the blind, to let the oppressed go free, to proclaim the year of the Lord's favour.'

When you step into a railway station, you see an overhead sign listing the destinations of the day's trains. Read down the list and your mind will be taken to distant scenes and far horizons. As you wait on the platform and a train prepares to move off, the platform sign will list a string of stops along the route. Jump on board and you will be taken there.

When Jesus reads from the Old Testament in the synagogue, the text seems rather like a departure board for his ministry. As we follow Luke's Gospel, here are the scenes we shall see, the direction in which the Gospel journey will take us, and the signs that will mark the way.

There is a sense of the Spirit at large and at work. The powerful presence of God stirs in Jesus, to breathe healing and hope into other people. Jesus is in touch with heaven, animated and anointed by God's touch. He is a Messiah in Israel and his anointing strengthens him to spread goodness and blessing to the communities he visits. Bruised and broken people discover new possibility and promise, and many find fresh confidence in God.

The Old Testament text is from Isaiah 61. We don't know if it was listed on a calendar of readings, or if Jesus just chose it himself, but the words obviously meant much to him. This passage described his ministry and it still sets out the service Christians are called to give in his name.

Prayer
*God of mercy, help me to see where your word and your love
can change lives for good.*

JP

Turbulent preacher

Then [Jesus] began to say to them, 'Today this scripture has been fulfilled in your hearing'... And he said, 'Truly I tell you, no prophet is accepted in the prophet's hometown. But the truth is, there were many widows in Israel in the time of Elijah... yet Elijah was sent to none of them except to a widow at Zarephath in Sidon...' When they heard this, all in the synagogue were filled with rage. They got up, drove him out of the town, and led him to the brow of the hill on which their town was built, so that they might hurl him off the cliff. But he passed through the midst of them and went on his way.

Jesus' synagogue visit certainly upset the local mood. First, he read from Isaiah, then he told people that the ancient text described him. Coming from a local boy, it produced a degree of scepticism, to say the least. There were surely people present that day who had wiped his nose as a baby, watched him playing in the street as a child and waited for him to settle down as a pillar of their community. Instead, he had wandered off and come back as some sort of prophet.

Worse was to come. In the days of Elijah and Elisha, Jesus said, God healed and helped people from outside Israel, even though many within the land needed care, too. Would Nazareth now be so wary about Jesus that the same would happen again? Would they miss the point of his message, while strangers and Gentiles discovered the grace of Israel's God?

It made people furious. Nazareth stands on a high ridge and in several places the ground slopes very steeply down. One particular site—the 'Hill of Precipitation'—has been marked by Christians over the centuries as the place where Jesus was almost killed. It is surely more important, though, to respond to the message of this incident rather than seek the exact spot. Are we welcoming or wary when God challenges us? Are our vision and horizon broad when we think of places God means to reach with the gospel?

Prayer
Lord Jesus Christ, please help me to welcome and reflect your good news in the place where I live.

Bible stories rediscovered: Noah's ark

It was the primary school highlight—*Captain Noah and his Floating Zoo*. Our elder daughter was Mrs Noah, the leading female role—at least until her best friend Ellie perched precariously atop the stepladder to play God. Our younger daughter was the West Wind—when she blew, the flood was gone!

The songs were great, the animal effects amazing. It reinforced the Sunday school realities: dramatic story, lots of animals and the rainbow—ideal for craftwork and colouring in. There's just that slightly awkward part… when God destroys the entire human race.

So let's revisit the story, now that we have outgrown Sunday school, and wrestle with what it has to say to adults living in the 21st century.

There are clearly two big questions. First, how historical is this story? Did a 600-year-old man *really* build a boat and survive a global catastrophic flood? Some would argue that the story could be literally true, but is believing that essential to its meaning? For the writer, the known world was actually just a small percentage of the globe, though many other ancient civilisations have flood disaster narratives. All who experience natural disasters will wonder why they happen and what they mean. My guess is that the folk memory of a real catastrophe was handed down, informing people's understanding of their own existence—and God.

The story is written in a highly stylised prose form mirrored around a central point. It starts and finishes with Noah doing the right thing (Genesis 6:9–12; 8:20–22). God tells Noah to build the ark—and to leave it (6:13–22; 8:15–19). The rain starts and the waters rise; the waters recede and dry up (7:11–24; 8:1–5). At the heart of story are the words 'God remembered Noah' (8:1).

So, the style reflects the story's purpose and focus, which is to answer the second big question: what is God like? The original readers lived in a culture far more exposed to untimely death and natural catastrophe than ours. In contrast to the other flood narratives of the time, the writer emphasises that the true God is not threatened by the flood, but sovereign over it; he judges, not capriciously, but on the basis of moral principle; and he is not indifferent to evil or suffering, but passionately committed to the salvation, restoration and continuation of his people and creation itself.

Stephen Rand

Broken-hearted

The Lord saw how great the wickedness of the human race had become on the earth, and that every inclination of the thoughts of the human heart was only evil all the time. The Lord regretted that he had made human beings on the earth, and his heart was deeply troubled. So the Lord said, 'I will wipe from the face of the earth the human race I have created—and with them the animals, the birds and the creatures that move along the ground—for I regret that I have made them.' But Noah found favour in the eyes of the Lord.

In the beginning, 'God saw all that he had made, and it was very good' (Genesis 1:31). Now God views the total corruption of his creation. The Fall, which brought sin and evil into the world, was not a hiccup in humankind's otherwise serene progress: it was crippling, total and complete. The 'inclination'—the tendency, the orientation—went only one way: towards evil. The 'thoughts'—the plans and schemes—were focused on selfishness. That is not a description of individual failings so much as a systemic failure. At the heart of the problem was that of the human heart; it was broken.

God's heart was broken, too. This translation uses quite gentle language for what is deep emotion. 'Regretted' is a word tied up with lament and grief, while 'deeply troubled' is a phrase that is also used for grief, torture and pain. If you have been a parent, you may understand a little the pain of a Father who sees his children rebelling against everything good.

God is not revealed as a potter who makes a mistake and decides to squash the clay to start again. Neither is he taken by surprise by sin. Rather, he shares in the pain it causes and is resolved, out of compassion, to intervene. There will be judgment, but there will also be a new start: one man carries the hope for a new creation.

The story of Noah's ark is the earliest version of the Bible's great story: the God whose mercy is revealed in the face of awful sin and terrible judgment.

Reflection

How much does the reality of evil in our world break my heart and make me determined to 'act justly and love mercy' (Micah 6:8)?

SR

The walk of faith

> This is the account of Noah and his family. Noah was a righteous man, blameless among the people of his time, and he walked faithfully with God. Noah had three sons: Shem, Ham and Japheth.

Here is the ray of hope cutting through the gloom. God's love and mercy will be vested in an individual; salvation will come through a man who is righteous and blameless and the human race will be rescued from destruction.

One sign that our own generation is corrupt is that being described as 'righteous' is probably seen as a negative. It simply means, of course, doing what is right. The Hebrew word used here can also be translated as 'justice'. This one word embodies the whole of God's concern for right living, of doing the right thing in relationship to God, our family, community and nation. God wants us to do what is right in our private life, public life, home, church, in the marketplace and in public service.

Noah did the right thing, walking faithfully with God. In fact, that undoubtedly helped him to do the right thing as it's easier to do what God wants when we spend time with him.

Walking implies journey, companionship, purpose. God walked with Adam in the Garden of Eden and still wants to walk with his descendants. He made us for relationship and he made us for a purpose. He wants to share his life with us so that we can share it with others—in all its fullness.

Noah's walk was full of faith. So many Christians only want to follow Jesus within their own boundaries. It takes faith to step outside those boundaries—whether they are geographical, social or relate to traditions. Don't settle for a stroll in the park when a trailblazing, mountain-climbing hike is on offer! Faith is essential if we are to continue walking when we do not know what will be around the corner… except that we know the God who walks with us can be trusted.

Prayer
Loving Father, thank you for inviting me to share my journey with you.
Give me the faith to follow you wherever you want me to go and the
strength to do the right thing every step of the way. Amen

SR

GENESIS 6:13–17 (NIV, ABRIDGED)

Building the lifeboat

God said to Noah, 'I am going to put an end to all people. They have filled the earth with their harmful acts. You can be sure that I am going to destroy both them and the earth. So make yourself an ark out of cypress wood. Make rooms in it. Cover it with tar inside and out. Here is how I want you to build it. The ark has to be 450 feet long. It has to be 75 feet wide and 45 feet high. Make a roof for it… I am going to bring a flood on the earth… Everything on earth will die.'

There is an awful contrast between the pronouncement of destruction and the detailed boatbuilding instructions. It is hard to imagine how Noah must have felt as this speech unfolded. He must have been aware of the evil all around him. Perhaps he had wondered if things could go on as they were… now he knew.

The flood is a highly symbolic—as well as a final—act of judgment. The writer explains that the earth itself has been corrupted by the corrupt behaviour of its inhabitants, so now they—and the earth itself—are to be cleansed.

This revelation is consistent with what the reader of Genesis has already been told about God. The Garden of Eden was where God's response to human sin was first spelled out: death was the price of failure to meet God's standards and that failure impacted the whole created order. Paul sums this up in Romans 8:22: 'the whole creation has been groaning as in the pains of childbirth.'

With justice and judgment, though, there comes mercy. The ark was the sign of God's intention to give the world a new start. With no sails, no oars, no engine, it could only float; it was not under any human control, but entirely dependent on God.

The Hebrew word for 'ark' appears in just one other story—when it is used for the basket in which the baby Moses was placed. That was a tiny 'lifeboat'; Noah's ark was an enormous ship. Both carried the future, God's way of escape; symbols of hope in the face of judgment.

Reflection

We have no idea how long Noah took to build the ark—perhaps he faced
ridicule for years—but 'By faith Noah… built an ark' (Hebrews 11:7).
May God grant us the faith to persevere.

SR

The covenant

[God said] 'But I will establish my covenant with you, and you will enter the ark—you and your sons and your wife and your sons' wives with you. You are to bring into the ark two of all living creatures, male and female, to keep them alive with you. Two of every kind of bird, of every kind of animal and of every kind of creature that moves along the ground will come to you to be kept alive. You are to take every kind of food that is to be eaten and store it away as food for you and for them.' Noah did everything just as God commanded him.

A new word appears! Here is the first mention in the Bible of a 'covenant'—a vital key to our understanding of God. It is a difficult word. Books have been written on its meaning and significance. It has a hint of a legal agreement about it, but it is not referring to a negotiated settlement where two parties sit down, draw up terms and then shake hands on it. This is God's initiative, the Creator setting out the terms for his creation.

It is a promise made by the living God, so it is completely solid and reliable. It is rooted in God's consistency and unfailing commitment. The pledge of relationship and life is implicit in the account of creation and here it is made explicit and, however desperate the reality of judgment, the commitment to relationship and life remains.

The ark is a provision for the covenant pledge to continue to the next stage and the food needs to be there so that the promise can and will be sustained. That is the story of the Bible as a whole, from Noah to Abraham, through Moses and David to Jesus himself and then to the end of time. God has made a commitment to the whole of the human race, the whole of creation. It is a pledge of love and life. No judgment will be allowed to snuff it out.

Prayer

Thank you, loving Father, for your commitment to us and your promise of life to all who believe. Thank you that you keep your promises. Amen

SR

Animal welfare

And Noah and his sons and his wife and his sons' wives entered the ark to escape the waters of the flood. Pairs of clean and unclean animals, of birds and of all creatures that move along the ground, male and female, came to Noah and entered the ark, as God had commanded Noah. And after the seven days the flood-waters came on the earth.

I love the film *Amazing Grace*, the story of William Wilberforce and his battle to end the transatlantic slave trade. I'm fascinated by its opening scene. You hear the sound of a whip and imagine that the horror of slavery is about to be revealed. Then you see that it is a horse, unable to pull a cart further, that is on the receiving end of two men's rage. Wilberforce intervenes to save it from its tormentors. This is not just a metaphor for the brutality of slavery. Wilberforce was known as a keen supporter of animal welfare, too, and helped set up the Society for the Prevention of Cruelty to Animals—now the RSPCA, as Queen Victoria was so impressed by its work that she allowed it to become Royal.

Adam named all the animals and Noah was instructed to ensure the survival of the animal kingdom: they mattered. They were included in the covenant we were thinking about yesterday, too. Sadly, Christians have lost the reputation Francis of Assisi and Wilberforce had for being concerned about animal as well as human welfare. It is a vital aspect of our God-given role as stewards of creation. The way we exercise our dominion over animals says something about how we value God's creation.

The Bible clearly teaches that human beings are distinct from the animal kingdom, uniquely made in his image and able to relate to him. We must also be clear that this doesn't give us a licence to exploit, ignore or mistreat creatures that God has made. What would we think of children who wilfully damaged something precious given to them by their father?

Reflection

If you have men who will exclude any of God's creatures from the shelter of compassion and pity, you will have men who will deal likewise with their fellow men.

Francis of Assisi (1182–1226)

SR

An act of God

For forty days the flood kept coming on the earth, and as the waters increased they lifted the ark high above the earth... The waters rose and covered the mountains to a depth of more than fifteen cubits... Every living thing on the face of the earth was wiped out; human beings and animals and the creatures that move along the ground and the birds were wiped from the earth. Only Noah was left, and those with him in the ark. The waters flooded the earth for a hundred and fifty days.

This was a catastrophic event. We cannot shy away from the horror revealed in these verses, which are repeatedly insistent about the totality of the destruction. I have never experienced a natural disaster, but I've seen their impact. I've sat stunned in the presence of a man who held on to his son with his teeth while the rest of his family were swept away. The images of tsunami and earthquake never fail to shock—nor should they.

The writer here is describing the first great natural disaster—and sees it as an act of God. But the theology of it is very clear: the whole creation has been corrupted by human sin. Natural disasters are not vengeful acts of God against specific people or nations; they are the outworking of the way sin has impacted the whole working of the universe.

Even in our time, we see the penalty of sin being worked out in the impact of disasters. The poor are pushed to the margins, most vulnerable to the devastation of floods and other disasters. It is not the homes of the wealthy, by and large, that are washed away or crumble into dust.

The number and severity of natural disasters are growing. This is one facet of the impact of climate change, brought on by the inability of the wealthiest nations of the world to control their insatiable demand for energy. The world's most vulnerable people are already paying the price. Gandhi was right: the world has enough for everyone's need, but not for everyone's greed.

Prayer

Lord God, we cry out for mercy for those facing suffering and experiencing bereavement because of natural disasters. We pray for your blessing on all those who bring relief to them. Amen

SR

God remembers

But God remembered Noah and all the wild animals and the livestock that were with him in the ark, and he sent a wind over the earth, and the waters receded. Now the springs of the deep and the floodgates of the heavens had been closed, and the rain had stopped falling from the sky... At the end of the hundred and fifty days the water had gone down, and on the seventeenth day of the seventh month the ark came to rest on the mountains of Ararat. The waters continued to recede... and on the first day of the tenth month the tops of the mountains became visible.

Here is the turning point of the whole story: 'God remembered Noah'. Wrongdoing was rife, God's judgment was pronounced, the rains fell, the flood levels rose and disaster overtook the human race, but then the waters receded. What happened was not just the inevitable progression of a random weather pattern; it was an act of God, just as the flood had been an act of God and the original creation had been an act of God.

Do you remember how it all started? 'Now the earth was formless and empty, darkness was over the surface of the deep, and the Spirit of God was hovering over the waters' (Genesis 1:2). There had been water before there was land. Now the water had once again overcome the land. Creation had been reversed, but chaos was not to rule again. The Creator began the process of re-creation and it started with Almighty God remembering a friend. He brought Noah to mind... and the waters receded.

Have you ever used the phrase 'I'm in over my head'? You may even feel that this is your experience right now, but, remember, however high the waters, however deep the despair, you are not forgotten; you, too, are remembered.

Reflection

My father used to sing with a male voice praise choir. Occasionally I still nostalgically play an old CD of them singing an ancient hymn that includes the lines, 'Torrents of sin and of anguish sweep o'er my sinking soul, and I perish, I perish, dear Master. Oh, hasten and take control!' Then the vast choir sing, as gently and reassuringly as they can, the response from Jesus: 'Peace, be still.'

GENESIS 8:6–11 (TNIV, ABRIDGED)

The dove of peace

After forty days Noah opened a window he had made in the ark and sent out a raven, and it kept flying back and forth until the water had dried up from the earth. Then he sent out a dove to see if the water had receded from the surface of the ground. But the dove could find nowhere to perch because there was water over all the surface of the earth; so it returned to Noah in the ark... He waited seven more days and again sent out the dove from the ark. When the dove returned to him in the evening, there in its beak was a freshly plucked olive leaf! Then Noah knew that the water had receded from the earth.

Yesterday we noted that 'God remembered Noah'. Today, people will remember those in the armed services who died in battle, although I have never forgotten one Remembrance Day service that widened the focus to include all who have given their life for the sake of others—relief workers, police officers, members of the emergency services.

There are two birds in today's reading. The raven feeds on carrion. It would be the first to find food in the gruesome aftermath of disaster, whether the horror of war or the mud-filled debris of flooding. The dove, however, eats seeds and fruit. It feeds on life and the promise of life rather than death. Noah's dove returned to the ark the second time with an olive leaf, linking what have become two powerful symbols of peace, but peace was not the obvious reference point for Noah in his situation. He saw the olive leaf in the dove's beak as evidence that the water had receded. Life could begin again. This is perhaps where the link with peace begins.

We often define peace as an absence of war. The Bible gives us God's perspective on peace, that it is about well-being, a positive and dynamic experience of relationship between an individual and fellow human beings, the Creator and his creation. Noah saw in the beak of the dove a sign that all this was once again possible.

Reflection

As we remember the dead today, let us commit ourselves to 'make every effort to do what leads to peace' (Romans 14:19): the peace that Jesus described as life in all its fullness (John 10:10).

SR

GENESIS 8:13, 15–17 (TNIV)

Be fruitful

By the first day of the first month of Noah's six hundred and first year, the water had dried up from the earth. Noah then removed the covering from the ark and saw that the surface of the ground was dry... Then God said to Noah, 'Come out of the ark, you and your wife and your sons and their wives. Bring out every kind of living creature that is with you—the birds, the animals, and all the creatures that move along the ground—so they can multiply on the earth and be fruitful and increase in number on it.'

The writer is clear who is in charge of this salvation journey. Noah observes that the ground is dry, but it is God who tells him when to leave the ark. All the voyagers must have been itching to be back on dry land, but Noah knew that he had been directed into the ark, so he waited to be directed out of it. Many have found waiting for God to be an irritating or even painful experience; others have discovered that impatience can spell disaster.

The directive to disembark is accompanied by the instruction first given to Adam in Genesis 1:28: 'Be fruitful.' There is a key point of biblical teaching here: salvation is not an end in itself, it is for a purpose. God had rescued Noah so that his purpose for creation could be fulfilled. Why do so many Christians imagine that the point of their faith is to be saved? Surely we are saved so that we can live life as God intended, fulfilling his purposes, blessing others. We are saved for fruitfulness.

The world he created was meant to be populated. Now there are over six billion people in the world, we worry about the burden that human existence places on the planet.

I am convinced that children are a blessing and every child should have the opportunity to experience life as a blessing. If the effort made to reduce the growth of the human population was applied to reducing human poverty, then the average size of families would decrease, the rate of population growth would be reduced and more children would indeed experience life as God intended.

Prayer

May our lives be marked by the fruitfulness of the Spirit and
may our world be marked by God's blessing.

SR

God provides

Then Noah built an altar to the Lord and, taking some of all the clean animals and clean birds, he sacrificed burnt offerings on it. The Lord smelled the pleasing aroma and said in his heart: 'Never again will I curse the ground because of human beings, even though every inclination of the human heart is evil from childhood. And never again will I destroy all living creatures, as I have done. As long as the earth endures, seedtime and harvest, cold and heat, summer and winter, day and night will never cease.'

It seems very strange that the first thing Noah does with his rescued animals is to sacrifice some of them! This, though, is a highly symbolic part of the story. Sacrifice indicates homage and commitment to God, that the one who had saved Noah from judgment was to be put first. It was a sign of the new creation, a new start.

In the Babylonian flood story, the gods ended the flood because they were hungry—no one was sacrificing animals, so they were not eating. Here, God is not looking for food, but he appreciates the aroma of the sacrifice that has been offered in recognition of the fact that creation belongs to him. Paul expresses our calling to sacrifice like this: 'Live a life of love, just as Christ loved us and gave himself up for us as a fragrant offering and sacrifice to God' (Ephesians 5:2).

The sacrifice prompts God to make a promise. Despite knowing that the human heart has not changed, in his mercy he guarantees that the fundamental sustenance of human existence will never again be withdrawn. I once sat with an elder of a church in a remote part of Burkina Faso in West Africa. The people there were in the midst of a famine, surviving on leaves, berries and roots scavenged from the bushes. I asked the elder if he accepted that the Bible was right when it said that God provides for his people. It seemed like an age until I had his answer as it was translated, first, into French, then into English. 'As long as there are leaves and berries on the trees, I know that God provides for his people', he said.

Prayer
Thank you, loving Father, for your promise of mercy and provision for the human race. Amen

SR

Made in the image of God

Then God blessed Noah and his sons, saying to them, 'Be fruit-ful and increase in number and fill the earth… Everything that lives and moves will be food for you. Just as I gave you the green plants, I now give you everything… And from each human being, too, I will demand an accounting for the life of another human being. Whoever sheds human blood, by human beings shall their blood be shed; for in the image of God has God made humanity.'

Noah began the new creation by offering a sacrifice to acknowledge the Creator. God responded with a promise to sustain the new creation. Here, four principles of the new order are spelled out.

God blesses: this is the keynote of God's relationship with his people of the new start. The origins and meaning of the word 'blessing' are hard to pin down, but in this context it literally means saying good words to someone, wishing them well. When those words come from God, though, they have power. Do we long for God's blessing? Do we share God's blessings?

God provides: the truth is the same, but the outworking of it has changed. The human race is dependent on God for its survival, but he has given us everything for our daily sustenance. That now includes the animals. These verses make it clear that sin and judgment have left their mark: the relationship with the animal kingdom will not be the same. Animals will fear humans and, experience suggests, rightly so.

God demands accountability: one of Adam's children had killed the other. As the human race moves out on its second chance, God makes it clear that not only is murder completely unacceptable but also a murderer must be held to account. Human beings have to take respon-sibility for their own actions and for dealing justly with others.

Humankind is made in the image of God: in this new order, the basic principle from which all else flows is clearly stated: whatever the rav-ages of sin and judgment, human beings are made in the image of God. That's why each one is precious. I am precious… you are precious.

Prayer

Lord, help me to see your image in every person I meet—
and may they see your image in me.

SR

The sign of the rainbow

[God said] 'Whenever I bring clouds over the earth and the rainbow appears in the clouds, I will remember my covenant between me and you and all living creatures of every kind. Never again will the waters become a flood to destroy all life. Whenever the rainbow appears in the clouds, I will see it and remember the everlasting covenant between God and all living creatures of every kind on the earth.' So God said to Noah, 'This is the sign of the covenant I have established between me and all life on the earth.'

We love rainbows! For me, the rainbow never loses its beauty, mystery and fascination. Even when I half understand the science of the prism, that knowledge does not detract from the majestic reality of a rainbow in the sky.

There is something simple yet profound about the fact that rain is needed for us to see the sign that rain will never again flood the whole earth. Noah and his family may have been particularly glad of that reassurance. They must have found it difficult when the dark clouds appeared once again and the rain began to fall, but the rainbow would have brought them reassurance.

I had thought it was intended to remind us of God's promise not to destroy life on earth, but the verses are clear—it is there first to remind God of his promise. Of course it does both as, when we see it, we can be sure God sees it! That reinforces the reassurance.

Reminders are important, from sticky notes to knots in a handkerchief. Reminders of promises made are even more so. It might be a note in the diary promising to meet up or a ring on the finger symbolising that solemn vows have been made.

The rainbow is a promise that is all-embracing, all-inclusive—it is between God and 'all living creatures'. It is everlasting and unconditional. We have not deserved it, we can do nothing to deserve it, but we can be sure that God will keep his promise.

Prayer

Dear God, thank you for your promise—and the sign of that promise.
Help me to be a keeper of promises and make my life a sign of
your grace and goodness. Amen

SR

GENESIS 9:20–23 (TNIV)

Drunk and disorderly

Noah, a man of the soil, proceeded to plant a vineyard. When he drank some of its wine, he became drunk and lay uncovered inside his tent. Ham, the father of Canaan, saw his father's nakedness and told his two brothers outside. But Shem and Japheth took a garment and laid it across their shoulders; then they walked in backwards and covered their father's nakedness. Their faces were turned the other way so that they would not see their father's nakedness.

We go from the glory of the rainbow to a sordid family secret. This is a strange and difficult story, its interpretation dependent on understanding the culture of the ancient Middle East. Any conclusions have to be tentative, but there are some simple points to make.

The most obvious is the danger of drunkenness. There is no doubt that the wide availability of increasingly cheaper alcohol has had a significant impact on our society. I reflect, gladly, that my first experience of drunkenness as a student was so unpleasant that I was not keen to repeat it. As a teacher, I was baffled by the relish and pride with which the sixth-formers would discuss their excesses.

The Bible celebrates wine, but prohibits drunkenness. Like so many of the best things in life, wine can be abused as well as bring pleasure. Drunkenness leads to demeaning behaviour. It is sadly shocking to think of Noah, full of faith, the man who had obeyed God, now lying sprawled indecently because of drink.

It is in the family where the impact is felt. There was a great taboo in this society against a son seeing his father naked. Maybe Ham should not have discussed it with others, but Shem and Japheth displayed respect and inventiveness in finding a way to put right what had gone wrong. Families can be great; they can also be a source of abuse and pain. Incidents in childhood can send tentacles of influence far down the years into adulthood. In our homes, just as in our communities and our churches, we need God's love to be shown and shared.

Prayer
Pray for families blighted by drunkenness and alcoholism. Remember, too, those who seek to help people break their dependency.

SR

The family of nations

These are the clans of Noah's sons, according to their lines of descent, within their nations. From these the nations spread out over the earth after the flood.

This is the conclusion of a chapter that symbolically describes the nations—or tribes—of the world at this point in human history. Some of the names are readily recognisable, others have disappeared from the history and geography books altogether, but this simple verse tells us something profound: all the nations of the earth stemmed from Noah and his three sons. There was equal and common ancestry; all were interconnected. It is as if the writer wants to emphasise that this is the starting point for the story of Abraham.

When one nation was chosen to be God's people, it was not to single them out for blessing, but for service, to ensure that God's blessings were shared with all nations. 'God,' says Paul, 'announced the gospel in advance to Abraham: "All nations will be blessed through you"' (Galatians 3:8). This challenges one of the major sources of tension and violence in the world today. The assertion of ethnic superiority is all too common. We can be so ready to emphasise our differences that we forget what unites us, what binds us together in the web of life. We are all made in the image of God.

There is no room for racism in the life of a follower of Jesus. Too many Christians pray for missionaries working in other countries, then ignore or resent people from those counties who come to live next door. Our adoption into God's family creates a relationship that will last for eternity, shared with people of every tribe and nation. In our churches we must constantly strive to find positive ways to anticipate that reality.

It's wonderful that people can express their worship in their own culture, but we must also find ways to share in worship together across racial divides. It would be a sin as well as a tragedy if Sunday mornings in church turned to be the most segregated hour in our nation's life.

Prayer

Heavenly Father, thank you for the rainbow nation that is your Church across the world. Help your people to celebrate the diversity of culture and race within the Church in the context of unity. Amen

SR

Don't forget to renew your annual subscription to *New Daylight*! If you enjoy the notes, why not also consider giving a gift subscription to a friend or member of your family?

You will find a subscription order form overleaf.
New Daylight is also available from your local
Christian bookshop.

INDIVIDUAL SUBSCRIPTIONS

❏ Please send me a Bible reading resources pack
❏ I would like to take out a subscription myself (complete your name and address details only once)
❏ I would like to give a gift subscription (please complete both name and address sections below)

Your name _____

Your address _____

_____ Postcode _____

Tel _____ Email _____

Gift subscription name _____

Gift subscription address _____

_____ Postcode _____

Gift message (20 words max.) _____

_____

Please send *New Daylight* beginning with the January 2011 issue:

(please tick box)	UK	SURFACE	AIR MAIL
NEW DAYLIGHT	❏ £14.40	❏ £15.90	❏ £19.20
NEW DAYLIGHT 3-year sub	❏ £36.00		
NEW DAYLIGHT DELUXE	❏ £18.00	❏ £22.50	❏ £28.80
NEW DAYLIGHT daily email only	❏ £12.00 (UK and overseas)		
NEW DAYLIGHT email + printed	❏ £23.40	❏ £24.90	❏ £28.20

Confirm your email address _____

Please complete the payment details below and send, with appropriate payment, to: **BRF, 15 The Chambers, Vineyard, Abingdon OX14 3FE.**

Total enclosed £ _____ (cheques should be made payable to 'BRF')

Please charge my Visa ❏ Mastercard ❏ Switch card ❏ with £ _____

Card number ☐☐☐☐☐☐☐☐☐☐☐☐☐☐☐☐☐☐☐☐☐☐

Expires ☐☐☐☐ Security code ☐☐☐ Issue no (Switch only) ☐☐☐☐

Signature (essential if paying by credit/Switch) _____

1 Kings 5—8

These chapters in 1 Kings describe the building of Solomon's temple and palace. It's a good idea to read through them because the passages that follow are only representative of the full story and are often abridged. If you do, you may think, 'But this is all about an ancient building project. What, if anything, is going to be relevant to me?' It's a fair question and the answer, I think, lies in three connected areas.

First of all, when buildings are planned, they give 'concrete' form to our ideas, which is why different cultures build different-looking buildings and architectural styles go out of date. This connection between ideas and architecture is especially true when it comes to religious buildings and we can learn as much about ourselves from our reactions to them as we can about those who built them. As we reflect on Solomon's temple, we learn about not only his faith but also ours.

Second, neither the temple nor the palace existed to promote Solomon's power. Both were expressions of God's covenant relationship with his people. Solomon inherited the task of building the temple from his father. It took him seven years to complete it and 13 to finish his palace. These, then, were long-term projects, but, even so, they can only be understood in the light of Solomon's kingship under God. Human nature is recognisable across cultures and history and, when we look closely at the life of Solomon, we learn something about ourselves.

Third, the temple had a function: it was where sacrifices were made. If your church is anything like mine, from time to time, old chairs, office desks, elderly TV sets (that sort of thing) 'turn up'. They are usually unwanted items that their owners no longer want but can't bear to just throw away, so they give them to their local church. I've never been sure whether the giving of these old possessions is intended as some sort of sacrifice to God or not, but, if it is, these worn-out items are about as far from old covenant sacrifices as you can get. Sacrifices made to God then were always of the very best quality.

Are these chapters relevant to 21st-century Christians? They reflect covenant ideas, help us to consider human nature and challenge us to offer our very best to God, so I, for one, would say yes!

David Robertson

Working in partnership

Solomon sent back this message to Hiram: '… I intend, therefore, to build a temple for the Name of the Lord my God… So give orders that cedars of Lebanon be cut for me. My men will work with yours, and I will pay you for your men whatever wages you set. You know that we have no one so skilled in felling timber as the Sidonians.' When Hiram heard Solomon's message, he was greatly pleased and said, 'Praise be to the Lord today, for he has given David a wise son to rule over this great nation.' … The Lord gave Solomon wisdom, just as he had promised him. There were peaceful relations between Hiram and Solomon, and the two of them made a treaty.

Solomon asked God for wisdom (1 Kings 3:9–12) and his prayer was answered. Here we see his wisdom in action, not in some pithy, penetrating remark, but in a mixture of flattery and practicality.

Most people enjoy praise and King Hiram was no different. When Solomon, his neighbour, waxed lyrical about his craftsmen, Hiram was so pleased that he not only agreed to Solomon's request but also provided materials and labour at a discount! All the payment he required was food for the palace (1 Kings 5:3–9).

There was, however, another layer to Solomon's flattery: he was simply telling the truth. The Hebrew people, with their history of nomadic herding, knew very little about woodworking, but the Sidonians (a seafaring, boat-building people) did. When the Hebrews worked alongside the Sidonians, they were apprenticed to them and so learned their skills. The result of Solomon's wisdom was a peace treaty with a neighbour and Hebrew master craftsmen.

These days, churches are increasingly thinking about partnership working—joining forces with secular organisations for the benefit of their communities. Although some Christians welcome such partnerships, others feel very nervous, fearing that the message of Christ will be compromised by secular ideas or practices. Today's reading shows that when partnership working is appropriate, it benefits everyone. It is also nothing new.

Reflection

'For whoever is not against us is for us' (Mark 9:40).

DR

Labour and reward

King Solomon conscripted labourers from all Israel—thirty thousand men. He sent them off to Lebanon in shifts of ten thousand a month, so that they spent one month in Lebanon and two months at home. Adoniram was in charge of the forced labour. Solomon had seventy thousand carriers and eighty thousand stonecutters in the hills, as well as thirty-three hundred overseers who supervised the project and directed the work. At the king's command they removed from the quarry large blocks of quality stone to provide a foundation of dressed stone for the temple. The skilled workers of Solomon and Hiram and those from Gebal cut and prepared the timber and stone for the building of the temple.

At first glance, this looks like slave labour, which raises all kinds of questions about the ethical foundations on which the temple was laid. The reality was different. At that time in Israel's history, tax was in part collected through servitude, so, for a certain number of weeks each year, the Hebrew men worked for the public good. Those who worked on the temple were not pressed into service in the sense that they could have been working at home instead—if they had not been doing this, they would have been working on some other public scheme.

At the heart of today's reading is an unexpected truth. The temple might have been Solomon's temple, but, over the years, it was the people who built it. Once it had been completed we can imagine vast numbers of Israelite men coming with their families (as part of their religious duties) and saying with pride, 'You see that wall? I built that!' That sense of ownership would have been a byproduct of servitude and, therefore, unexpected, but real nonetheless.

In churches today, it's not unheard of for individuals to moan about congregational apathy—that no one else shares their sense of urgency about youth work, buildings maintenance, evangelism or whatever. Today's passage reminds us that if an individual builds (or provides something for others), that individual alone will own it, but if a group or team of people build it, they will all own it.

Reflection

For Christians to express unity, they have to work together.

DR

House and home

The temple that King Solomon built for the Lord was sixty cubits long, twenty wide and thirty high... In building the temple, only blocks dressed at the quarry were used, and no hammer, chisel or any other iron tool was heard at the temple site while it was being built... The word of the Lord came to Solomon: 'As for this temple you are building, if you follow my decrees, carry out my regulations and keep all my commands and obey them, I will fulfil through you the promise I gave to David your father. And I will live among the Israelites and will not abandon my people Israel.'

From the descriptions that we have of Solomon's temple, we know that it was about the same size and shape as a sports hall. Rows of columns supported the roof and, as well as the columned, central area, there were other rooms built into the side walls. Had the temple survived, it would not seem (to our 21st-century eyes) particularly large or impressive and some might regard the wallcarvings as 'fussy'.

What we might think of the temple is not the point. Solomon constructed the most advanced, impressive building that he could as a tribute to God and God accepted his offering. His word to Solomon makes it clear, however, that his chief concerns were the people's behaviour and their ongoing relationship with him.

This reminds me of the contrast between families that are focused on maintaining their houses (keeping them tidy and perfect) and those focused on their homes (making them happy and safe). My personal observation is that while the latter can be tidy or untidy with little positive or negative effect, the former can end up emotionally dry.

It would be too strong to say that Solomon built a house of God whereas God wanted a home among his people. Solomon's intentions were good, but, as time passed, God's criticism of his people was often, 'You keep my house immaculately, but you neglect the relationship that makes us a family!' God forbid that he should ever level that criticism at us.

Prayer

Lord, may the church always be a home, not a house, of God.

DR

1 KINGS 6:19, 23, 27–30 (NIV)

An encouragement to worship

He prepared the inner sanctuary within the temple to set the ark of the covenant of the Lord there... In the inner sanctuary he made a pair of cherubim of olive wood, each ten cubits high... He placed the cherubim inside the innermost room of the temple, with their wings spread out. The wing of one cherub touched one wall, while the wing of the other touched the other wall, and their wings touched each other in the middle of the room. He overlaid the cherubim with gold. On the walls all round the temple, in both the inner and outer rooms, he carved cherubim, palm trees and open flowers. He also covered the floors of both the inner and outer rooms of the temple with gold.

My first introduction to lavish church architecture was on holiday in Spain with my family when I was ten. We visited a cathedral that I found impressive from the outside, but, when we went inside, I changed my mind. Everything was covered in gold and bright colours and the only other place I'd seen anything like it was on fairground rides. It just didn't seem right to me that a church should look like that. I have to confess that I still feel much the same about 'church bling' and I suspect that I would have found Solomon's temple gaudy.

You may share my taste or you may not. Some people love bright colours and loathe plain churches, which they find dowdy. Some hate old, traditional buildings with the same passion that others reserve for modern structures. Even in the average, settled, congregation there will be some (or many) who would prefer the architecture and decoration of their church to be different.

Satisfying personal taste is not the overall aim of religious architecture, though. Solomon designed his temple to encourage the people of his culture to seek God. Church architecture and decoration only matter in as much as they encourage the people of any culture to seek God. It may be worth looking at your own church building with a fresh eye.

Reflection

Does my church building speak of the living God in a way that the people of my culture can understand?

DR

Solomon's palace

It took Solomon thirteen years... to complete the construction of his palace. He built the Palace of the Forest of Lebanon a hundred cubits long, fifty wide and thirty high, with four rows of cedar columns supporting trimmed cedar beams. It was roofed with cedar above the beams that rested on the columns—forty-five beams, fifteen to a row... He built the throne hall, the Hall of Justice, where he was to judge, and he covered it with cedar from floor to ceiling. And the palace in which he was to live, set farther back, was similar in design. Solomon also made a palace like this hall for Pharaoh's daughter, whom he had married.

When Solomon built his palace, he made it a multipurpose building. It was his centre of administration, the place where law was made and where he received foreign dignitaries. It was his version of Parliament, Whitehall, the Old Bailey and Buckingham Palace all in one (and it was next door to the temple). He also built luxurious living quarters for himself and his family, but the palace was primarily a place of work.

In our democratic culture, we have a monarch, a prime minister, a chancellor of the exchequer, a chief constable, a lord chief justice and a foreign secretary. We are used to a variety of people fulfilling these different roles, but Solomon, in his culture, was the king and he played all these roles. He held ultimate power in every aspect of government and was answerable only to God.

Whenever the Bible speaks of the 'kingdom of God', it is referring to this kind of kingship. God (or the Messiah) is a centralised king who holds ultimate power in every aspect of life. That is why it is so important to us that God reveals himself in Jesus to be loving, forgiving and accepting. When we declare that 'Jesus is our King', however, it may lose something in translation. Some Christians may think that this means a king in the same way that Queen Elizabeth II is a queen—part of the shared system—but we are, in fact, declaring that Jesus is a king to whom everyone is subject in every aspect of life (Romans 14:11).

Prayer
Lord, you are my king; I kneel before you.

DR

1 KINGS 7:13–21 (NIV, ABRIDGED)

Columns

King Solomon sent to Tyre and brought Huram... [who] was highly skilled and experienced in all kinds of bronze work... He cast two bronze pillars... two capitals of cast bronze to set on the tops of the pillars... [and] a network of interwoven chains festooned the capitals on top of the pillars... He made pomegranates in two rows encircling each network... The capitals on top of the pillars in the portico were in the shape of lilies... [and] above the bowl-shaped part next to the network were the two hundred pomegranates in rows all around. He erected the pillars at the portico of the temple.

If there's an image that sums up Solomon's culture, it's columns. In his day, building techniques were rudimentary and if he wanted to build a large building, he needed columns to hold up the roof—and lots of them! Columns were needed to support the temple in the same way that people were needed to support Solomon's kingship. His culture was communal.

Our culture is individual. We admire self-reliance and prize personal space so much that we distance ourselves from other people even when we are in a crowd. Earphones are a badge of that individuality! No one in Solomon's culture could be individualistic in the way that we can, but, then, no one in his culture could be lonely in the way that many people in our culture are.

Interestingly, despite our individualistic culture, the word 'community' is used often. Sometimes it means 'interest groups', or 'residents', or 'targets of social action', but it rarely means 'community' in any sense that Solomon would have understood. His was a 'covenant community' where belonging and contributing were two sides of the same coin.

In the same way, the 'Christian community' isn't primarily an interest group or a gathering of residents. It may focus on social action, but it exists because it is a covenant community. God in Christ seeks us individually (Luke 15:4), but, once we have been 'found', our faith is corporate (John 10:16). We each become a column in the kingdom of God—Christians together.

Reflection
A building supported by one column will soon topple.

DR

A ceremonial pool

[Huram] made the Sea of cast metal, circular in shape, measuring ten cubits from rim to rim and five cubits high. It took a line of thirty cubits to measure round it. Below the rim, gourds encircled it—ten to a cubit. The gourds were cast in two rows in one piece with the Sea. The Sea stood on twelve bulls, three facing north, three facing west, three facing south and three facing east. The Sea rested on top of them, and their hindquarters were towards the centre. It was a handbreadth in thickness, and its rim was like the rim of a cup, like a lily blossom. It held two thousand baths.

This ceremonial bath was built at the temple entrance. To make a model of it, you would need to raid a farmyard set for twelve plastic bulls lying down with their legs tucked under them, sphinx-like. If you put the bulls in sets of three facing out towards the four points of the compass and balanced a bowl on their backs you would get some idea of what the bath looked like. The real thing was made of bronze, about 2 metres high, 4.5 metres across and held around 45,464 litres of water. According to 2 Chronicles 4:6, this was where the temple priests bathed as a ritual before attending to their duties.

The Sea was placed by the temple door because of the holiness of God. The temple was thought of as God's dwellingplace and most people who went there went to fulfil the commands of the old covenant. They went to offer the sacrifices specified in the Law and many came to make sin offerings because they knew that they had done wrong. When they arrived at the temple, the first thing they would see, before they even went inside, was the Sea (with, most probably, priests washing themselves). It was a vivid reminder that the priests who would shortly accept the sacrifices on God's behalf were themselves no cleaner spiritually than anyone else.

If we should ever fall into the trap of thinking that our church leaders are somehow holier than the members of the congregation, perhaps we should build a Sea outside our churches!

Reflection

In God's holy presence we are all on level ground.

DR

Bronze carts

[Huram] also made ten movable stands of bronze; each was four cubits long, four wide and three high. This is how the stands were made: they had side panels attached to uprights. On the panels between the uprights were lions, bulls and cherubim—and on the uprights as well… Each stand had four bronze wheels with bronze axles, and each had a basin resting on four supports, cast with wreaths on each side… Each stand had four handles, one on each corner, projecting from the stand… He also made the basins and shovels and sprinkling bowls. So Huram finished all the work he had undertaken for King Solomon in the temple of the Lord.

These ten stands held basins that were used for ritually washing the freshly butchered parts of sacrificial animals before they were burnt as offerings (2 Chronicles 4:6). Unlike the huge Sea, these stands were designed to be wheeled around the temple. Interestingly, more than one commentator has made the very practical observation that, once they were built (from bronze) and filled with water, they would probably have been too heavy to move. Bronze wheels and axles would not have been up to the job. 2 Chronicles 4:6 bears this out, suggesting that they ended up being permanently placed.

I find this fact very encouraging because every church that I've belonged to has had stands like these. Not actual bronze stands on wheels, of course, but ideas, projects, groups, events, storage solutions, building rejigs and so forth that never worked out as originally intended. The original vision was clear, everyone supported it, resources were found and the vision implemented, but it just didn't work. I could tell you about the evangelistic group that met in the pub and had a nice time but never evangelised, or the prayer room that was used mostly for meetings… but perhaps I'd better not!

The lesson from Solomon's temple onwards is that an idea might be right or wrong, but, unless you try it, you will never know. Maybe this Advent we could try something new, even if last time it did not really work out.

Prayer

Lord, give me the courage to keep putting ideas into practice.

DR

Terrier and inventory

All these objects that Huram made for King Solomon for the temple of the Lord were of burnished bronze. The king had them cast in clay moulds in the plain of the Jordan between Succoth and Zarethan. Solomon left all these things unweighed, because there were so many; the weight of the bronze was not determined… When all the work King Solomon had done for the temple of the Lord was finished, he brought in the things his father David had dedicated—the silver and gold and the furnishings—and he placed them in the treasuries of the Lord's temple.

In the Church of England, we are required to keep both a terrier and an inventory. This causes mild amusement every AGM when someone volunteers to take the terrier for a walk or give it a bowl of water! In fact, the terrier is just a list of everything each church owns that is immovable (the church hall, the organ and so forth), whereas the inventory lists everything that can be moved (service books, chairs, that sort of thing).

This passage is a kind of temple terrier and inventory, but there is a significant difference. In the present day, such lists are kept for insurance purposes, to determine the financial settlement in the event of a fire or theft. In effect, the terrier and inventory describe the wealth of the church. When Solomon's temple was built, though, the wealth (as determined by the weight of bronze, silver and gold used) was deliberately not recorded. Why?

Solomon, and the people, believed that the temple belonged to God. It was as grand as they could make it, decorated ornately and furnished lavishly, and it was their hope that God would make his home there and dwell among his people. The temple did not belong to Solomon, the builders or the people, so it was none of their business how much it was worth. To weigh God's bronze, silver and gold would be tantamount to coveting a neighbour's wealth, so they didn't do it.

The temple could have been a testimony to human achievement. It could have become a source of pride. Solomon wisely made sure that did not happen.

Reflection

'For where your treasure is, there your heart will be also' (Matthew 6:21).

DR

The ark of the covenant

The priests then brought the ark of the Lord's covenant to its place in the inner sanctuary of the temple, the Most Holy Place, and put it beneath the wings of the cherubim... There was nothing in the ark except the two stone tablets that Moses had placed in it at Horeb, where the Lord made a covenant with the Israelites after they came out of Egypt. When the priests withdrew from the Holy Place, the cloud filled the temple of the Lord. And the priests could not perform their service because of the cloud, for the glory of the Lord filled his temple. Then Solomon said, 'The Lord has said that he would dwell in a dark cloud; I have indeed built a magnificent temple for you, a place for you to dwell for ever.'

Now that the temple was finished, only one thing remained—to put the ark of the covenant, which had travelled with the Hebrew people since they left Egypt, in the most holy place. When that was done, with due ceremony and in the presence of the nation's leaders, the holiness of God filled the temple like a cloud. The sense of God's presence was so powerful that the priests were unable to go back inside.

This experience of God's holiness as a tangible cloud occurs from time to time in the Bible. It's called *shekinah* and was seen by Moses (Exodus 34:5) and Jesus' disciples (Matthew 17:5), and will be experienced by everyone at Jesus' second coming (Mark 14:62).

God makes himself known in the *shekinah* at specific times. It is right, then, to ask why God revealed his presence in this way to Solomon and the leaders of the people on that particular day. Was it because the temple was finished? Was it because it was suitably grand? Was it God's seal of approval on the bronze, gold and silver treasures? No; it was because the ark of the covenant was placed in the temple. God was affirming that the covenant was at the centre of his relationship with his people. Once the covenant was clearly the focus of the temple, God made himself known.

Reflection
God always has been, and still is, a God of covenant.

DR

1 KINGS 8:14–15, 19–20 (NIV, ABRIDGED)

Focus or location?

While the whole assembly of Israel was standing there, the king turned round and blessed them. Then he said: 'Praise be to the Lord, the God of Israel, who with his own hand has fulfilled what he promised with his own mouth to my father David… "You are not the one to build the temple, but your son, who is your own flesh and blood—he is the one who will build the temple for my Name." The Lord has kept the promise he made: I have succeeded David my father and now I sit on the throne of Israel, just as the Lord promised, and I have built the temple for the Name of the Lord, the God of Israel.'

The temple was completed not by the final building works but by God's revelation of himself within it. This is a lesson for any church building project—the time to celebrate is perhaps not when the builders move out and the ribbon is cut but when God first makes himself known to those using the new structure.

In today's reading, Solomon assumes the role of a high priest—addressing the people, blessing them and praising God on their behalf. In this moment of inspiration, he becomes a living prophecy, a prophetic precursor of another 'son of David' who will come later (Matthew 21:9)—the Messiah, who will be both king and priest for the people.

It's at this inspired moment that Solomon recognises the temple's limitations. As he says in 1 Kings 8:27, 'Will God really dwell on earth? The heavens, even the highest heaven, cannot contain you. How much less this temple I have built!' The temple will be a focus of God's covenant with his people, a point in time and space where sacrifices will be made and forgiveness granted, and God will 'dwell' there, but not in the sense that he will be confined by the building. God always has been, and always will be, involved in the daily lives of his people. His presence in the temple does not equate to his absence from everywhere else. Dwelling there does not mean that God is 'located' there. He is everywhere, with everyone, all the time.

Prayer
Lord, may I know you in every moment, in every place.

DR

God is known by name

Then Solomon stood before the altar of the Lord in front of the whole assembly of Israel, spread out his hands towards heaven and said: 'O Lord, God of Israel, there is no God like you in heaven above or on earth below—you who keep your covenant of love with your servants who continue wholeheartedly in your way... May your eyes be open towards this temple night and day, this place of which you said, "My Name shall be there," so that you will hear the prayer your servant prays towards this place... And forgive your people, who have sinned against you; forgive all the offences they have committed against you, and cause their conquerors to show them mercy.'

In most English translations, Solomon's prayer begins with, 'O Lord, God of Israel'. To us, this sounds like a formal mode of address, but, in Hebrew, Solomon addresses God by name. Yahweh tends to be translated as 'Lord', but it isn't a title, it's a name and that's why God's name shall be in the temple. He has made himself known by name and it is one of those that Solomon uses: Yahweh.

For God to give his name to his people was no small matter. In their culture, revealing your name was a sign of trust. Names were descriptive and chosen because of their meaning. For example, it was no accident that Jesus was given that name (Luke 1:31): it means 'saviour'. When God shared his name with his people it was part of the covenant. He was making himself known, describing himself and trusting them with that knowledge.

Although our culture is different, we too may be cautious of giving our names to strangers. When an aggressive person phones us and demands, 'Who's that?' we want to know if it's a genuine caller before we answer and, if it's a wrong number, we don't tell them. It's a matter of trust. The astonishing thing about God is that, even when his people proved untrustworthy, he kept trusting them. He kept his covenant promise. He forgave them and he has the power to do so because he is Yahweh.

Prayer

Lord, thank you that you make yourself known to us by name.

DR

The end of the exodus

'[These people] are your people and your inheritance, whom you brought out of Egypt, out of that iron-smelting furnace. May your eyes be open to your servant's plea and to the plea of your people Israel, and may you listen to them whenever they cry out to you. For you singled them out from all the nations of the world to be your own inheritance, just as you declared through your servant Moses when you, O Sovereign Lord, brought our ancestors out of Egypt.'

The completion of the temple, now that it has been filled with God's glory, marks the end of the exodus. When God led the people out of Egypt, they travelled with Moses for 40 years. During those years, what was to become temple worship was instituted (Exodus 25—30) but took place in the tabernacle, the tent they had made as a sign of the Lord's presence. When the people began to occupy the land that would become Israel, for many generations they were still primarily nomadic. Gradually they became farmers and traders and villages, towns and cities became the norm. Finally, with their third king, Solomon, their society was settled enough to warrant an administrative and religious centre (the palace and the temple). The days of wandering were over.

Solomon, in his prayer, recognised that this was a turning point in history. All that was temporary during the exodus was now permanent. When the people left Egypt, God's *shekinah* (glory) led them (Exodus 13:20–22). Now his *shekinah* would lead them into their future. The people were God's 'inheritance' or, to put it another way, the future, and God, by sharing his glory in the temple, had blessed that future.

The exodus was to be remembered, though. Within the stone temple, the Most Holy Place, where the ark was kept, was made of curtains. The Holy of Holies was like the tabernacle to remind the people that, although they had settled in the land, they were to still put their trust in the God who continued to lead them. It was right for them to put down roots, but, through their covenant faith, they would always move on spiritually.

Prayer
Lord, I am ready to move on in faith. Lead me.

DR

Walk in God's ways

[Solomon] stood and blessed the whole assembly of Israel in a loud voice, saying: 'Praise be to the Lord, who has given rest to his people Israel just as he promised. Not one word has failed of all the good promises he gave through his servant Moses. May the Lord our God be with us as he was with our ancestors; may he never leave us nor forsake us. May he turn our hearts to him, to walk in all his ways and to keep the commands, decrees and regulations he gave our ancestors... But your hearts must be fully committed to the Lord our God, to live by his decrees and obey his commands, as at this time.'

As Solomon concludes his prayer here, he reaffirms the covenant: Yahweh is their God; they are his people. God kept his promise: the nation was now free, a kingdom in its own right, the people were at rest in the land and God was with them. Now they needed to keep their side of the covenant so that, with hearts turned to God, they would walk in his ways, obedient to his commandments.

Many Christians regard the old covenant as rule-bound obedience expressed within a framework of brutal animal sacrifice. In truth, that is what it often became and what prophets such as Amos and Hosea spoke against. In fact, it was intended to be like a marriage (Isaiah 61:10; 62:5), an expression of God's love for his people and his desire that they might know him. Even Jesus made no criticism of the old covenant (Matthew 5:18), only of those who purported to interpret it (23:23–28).

The problem did not lie with the old covenant or with God but with people—with us. None of us has ever been able to keep the covenant as Solomon prayed that the people of God would. We ignore God's decrees and break his commands. That's why Jesus came to fulfil the old covenant and become, in himself, the new covenant (Matthew 5:17). It was in Christ that God revealed his love for us and his desire that we might know him and it is through Christ that we respond.

Reflection

Jesus has become for us righteousness, holiness and redemption
(1 Corinthians 1:30).

DR

Only the best

Then the king and all Israel with him offered sacrifices before the Lord. Solomon offered a sacrifice of fellowship offerings to the Lord: twenty-two thousand cattle and a hundred and twenty thousand sheep and goats. So the king and all the Israelites dedicated the temple of the Lord... So Solomon observed the festival at that time, and all Israel with him—a vast assembly, people from Lebo Hamath to the Wadi of Egypt. They celebrated it before the Lord our God for seven days and seven days more, fourteen days in all. On the following day he sent the people away. They blessed the king and then went home, joyful and glad in heart for all the good things the Lord had done for his servant David and his people Israel.

In our final reading, the temple, the focus of God's covenant with his people, begins its work. We may baulk at the scale of the butchery involved in its inauguration, but the sacrifices were an expression of God's ownership of the kingdom and a way of honouring God's ownership of the land. The people were settled, but it was God's land, not theirs, and, should they ever forget it, their sacrifices would remind them of it. The herds belonged to God and so did the grain, so it was right for the people to offer the first portion back to him. Moreover, everything sacrificed was of the best quality; God deserved nothing less.

As new covenant believers, our covenant with God is also expressed through sacrifice and Peter describes it in temple terms (1 Peter 2:4–7). In the new covenant, though, the temple is built from 'living stones' (believing people) and its focus is the self-sacrifice of Christ on the cross and the sacrifice in response of believers offering their lives back to God. This relationship is now the 'temple' where God dwells, where he makes himself known.

Solomon's temple was destroyed and then rebuilt by Zerubbabel (Ezra 1—6) before being replaced with Herod's temple. Little now remains in Jerusalem, but God's temple remains—it's you and me in Christ.

Prayer

Lord, you sacrificed your life for me; may I always sacrifice my best to you.

DR

Letters to the seven churches of Asia

Life can be difficult to understand. Personal, national and world events often leave us puzzled, confused and with lots of questions. What is it all about? What's really going on? Who can make sense of it all? Is there purpose and meaning to life? Can we be sure about anything?

The last book of the Bible holds a fascination for many of us, but it isn't the easiest to understand. The first three chapters are the focus of our readings over the next two weeks and are (thankfully!) the most straightforward. It is helpful, however, to have a sense of what the rest of the book is about to help us grasp the significance of these early chapters.

'Revelation' (or 'Apocalypse') simply means an unveiling. Things that were previously unknown are now being made known, what was hidden is now revealed: 'This is a revelation from Jesus Christ, which God gave him concerning the events that will happen soon' (Revelation 1:1, NLT). It is as if a curtain is drawn back and God says, 'Look at this!' Much of what is revealed deals with the spiritual realities that exist behind the scenes of life as we experience it. We are given a glimpse into the throne room of heaven and the throne is not empty. As we read in chapter four, verse two: 'I saw a throne in heaven and someone sitting on it!' The world has not been set in motion and left to its own devices—there is someone in charge in the control room of the universe.

My understanding of Revelation is that it is dealing with what we might call the time of the Church—the time stretching between Christ's first coming and his second coming. That was the time John was living in. It is the time *we* are living in. This book of the Bible encourages us to see our lives in the bigger context of God's rule and reign in the world and across the ages.

The great unveiling begins with a vision of the risen Christ and letters written to congregations of God's people—seven churches in Asia Minor (now Turkey). We will find that the messages to the churches back then are pertinent and relevant to the Church here and now.

Elaine Duncan

An astonishing letter

This is a revelation from Jesus Christ, which God gave him concerning the events that will happen soon. An angel was sent to God's servant John so that John could share the revelation with God's other servants... This letter is from John to the seven churches in the province of Asia. Grace and peace from the one who is, who always was, and who is still to come; from the seven spirits before his throne; and from Jesus Christ, who is the faithful witness to these things, the first to rise from the dead and the commander of all the rulers of the world... 'I am the Alpha and the Omega—the beginning and the end, says the Lord God. I am the one who is, who always was, and who is still to come, the Almighty One.'

We can easily skim over these opening verses and fail to grasp the magnitude of this unveiling from Jesus to his disciple, John. This revelation is from Jesus Christ and it is to his servants. Even the traditional greeting of 'grace and peace' is described as being from Jesus himself.

Christ's eternal character is emphasised twice in this opening section. The one who has already been, the one who is and the one who is also to come again, the beginning and the end, is speaking through his servant John. In a world that we experience as being full of uncertainty, this is a sure and certain description of Jesus. The first audience for this letter was living through immense turmoil. The Church was experiencing persecution and compromise was rife. Into this context came this amazing communication from the one who is 'commander of all the rulers of the world'.

Jesus is the Alpha and the Omega, the beginning and the end. This incredible statement, capturing the eternal existence of Jesus and his absolute centrality in the universe, is repeated at the end of Revelation (22:13). John is being reassured that he is in very safe hands.

Life can be uncertain for us, too—personally, in our communities, on the world stage. Do you need to know the steady, steadfast character of Jesus today?

Prayer
Lord Jesus, help me to hear you say 'grace and peace'
to me personally today.

ED

What a glorious sight!

'Write down what you see, and send it to the seven churches...'
When I turned to see who was speaking to me, I saw seven gold
lampstands. And standing in the middle of the lampstands was
the Son of Man... When I saw him, I fell at his feet as dead. But
he laid his right hand on me and said 'Don't be afraid! I am the
First and the Last. I am the living one who died. Look, I am alive
forever and ever! And I hold the keys of death and the grave.'

If you read the whole second half of Revelation 1, you will capture
something of the awesome nature of this vision given to John. We might
say today that he was 'gobsmacked'! The loud voice, the lamps on their
stands and this figure in the middle that John can hardly find words to
describe: 'His face was as bright as the sun in all its brilliance' (v. 16).

It is a scary vision, but strangely reassuring, too. John was in exile
and suffering for being a Christian, not on holiday on a Greek island.
In that context, he was worshipping God. Life was tough and demand-
ing—and he worshipped God. His future was uncertain—and he worshipped God. Then came the voice and the vision. Yes, the vision was
terrifying—so terrifying that John was in a state of collapse—but Jesus
gave him words of reassurance that again focus on his eternal existence
and victory over death. Have you ever been so overwhelmed with awe
as you consider Jesus that you have trembled? Often our visions of him
are too small to have such an effect!

John saw this awesome Jesus walking among seven lampstands,
holding seven stars. We are told that this signifies Jesus walking among
the churches. He holds the churches in his hands. He is indeed 'the
head of the church, which is his body' (Colossians 1:18).

Think of the congregation of Christ's people that you belong to. Is
there a tangible consciousness that you are together being in the hands
of Jesus? How might you encourage someone in your church community to think about that this week?

Prayer

Lord Jesus, help me to grow in confidence that you
hold the Church in your hands.

ED

Good thinking, Ephesus!

'Write this letter to the angel of the church in Ephesus. This is the message from the one who holds the seven stars in his right hand, the one who walks among the seven gold lampstands. I know all the things you do. I have seen your hard work and your patient endurance. I know you don't tolerate evil people. You have examined the claims of those who say they are apostles but are not. You have discovered they are liars. You have patiently suffered for me without giving up.'

Each letter to the individual churches follows a similar pattern. Each starts with a description of Jesus. Then the church is commended for something that it is getting right. This is usually followed by a criticism and a warning. Repentance is then urged. They end with a promise that relates either to the opening description of Jesus or to the vision of the city of God described towards the end of the book.

Ephesus was a thriving city, the main trade gateway into Asia Minor, and would have been a busy place with wealth and opulence clearly on display. It was the proud home of the temple of Artemis (Diana). Not an easy place to be a Christian! The church in Ephesus began when Paul visited the city and preached in the synagogue for three months, followed by a two-year stay, during which he preached daily (Acts 19). The church had definitely been thoroughly grounded in good teaching!

This background forms the basis for Jesus' commendation. The people have put in the hard work of learning and applied that learning to what others taught to work out what was true and false. Jesus was pleased with their efforts.

I spent many years working with students and was saddened to encounter many who were becoming experts in their area of study, but still at primary school level in their understanding of the Bible. We all need to be challenged about how much time and effort we put into learning for the sake of our jobs or hobbies compared with how much energy we put into knowing Jesus better by studying the Bible. The gospel engages our minds.

Prayer

Lord Jesus, open my mind to know and understand you better.

ED

Lost love

'But I have this complaint against you. You don't love me or each other as you did at first! Look how far you have fallen from your first love! Turn back to me again and work as you did at first. If you don't, I will come and remove your lampstand from its place among the churches... Anyone who is willing to hear should listen to the Spirit and understand what the Spirit is saying to the churches.'

Our reading yesterday showed us that the Christians in Ephesus were hardworking, doctrinally sound followers of Jesus. He has a serious complaint against them, though. As a result of all their hard work, hard thinking and hard perseverance, they had become hard! Somehow, love for Christ and love for one another had been lost along the way.

It happens so easily, doesn't it? Our zeal can take on a life of its own and a hard edge. It becomes detached from devotion to God and people. These early Christians had been busy defending themselves and the gospel from false teachers—and in the process lost their passion for the person of Jesus. The call to repentance suggests that their motives for working hard had become misplaced. Jesus is calling them to work as they did when they first knew him—that is, be motivated by love and devotion, not duty and a desire to be right.

Notice the criticism is that there was a lack of love for both Jesus and one another. When we spot that someone is teaching what is false, it is easy for us to not just reject the teaching but also the teacher. It is as important to be gracious as it is to be right.

Many of us will have had experience of love growing cold in a relationship. It does nothing to foster the growth of the relationship and can lead to a drifting apart. Jesus warns against this in relation to himself. If the church does not turn back to loving Christ again, then their lampstand will be removed—they will no longer be counted as one of his churches.

What about your relationship with Jesus and with your fellow Christians? Do you need a fresh inflow of Christ's love for you to rekindle your love for him and others?

Prayer

Warm my cold heart, O Lord, I pray.

ED

Smyrna suffers

'This is the message from the one who is the First and the Last, who died and is alive: I know about your suffering and your poverty—but you are rich!… Don't be afraid of what you are about to suffer. The Devil will throw some of you into prison and put you to the test. You will be persecuted for ten days. Remain faithful even when facing death, and I will give you the crown of life.'

The church in Smyrna receives the shortest letter of all, and there is no rebuke. Smyrna was a thriving, commercial city with everything going for it. The same could not be said of the church there. Persecution and poverty, hostility and hunger were the hallmarks of that church.

Today it is estimated that there are about 200 million Christians around the world who are facing direct persecution. Many more face less serious hostility, but hostility nonetheless. The short letter to the church in Smyrna holds much in the way of encouragement for those who are hard-pressed and struggling today.

Jesus first of all reminded them of his credentials for speaking to their situation—he is the one who died, suffered and experienced persecution at first hand. He was neither ignorant of their suffering—he knew that it was happening—nor did he fail to understand it. Then comes the incredible statement 'but you are rich!' I bet that made them stop in their tracks. In what ways were they rich?

Jesus seems to encourage taking a different perspective on their situation. He says that hardships can be viewed differently. They were rich because they knew the source of life itself. It really is only Jesus who can say, 'Don't be afraid of what you are about to suffer'. He reassured them that the suffering was to be limited ('ten days' was probably figurative rather than literal, however). He is the only one who can take us safely through the difficulties we experience in life and make us champions in the end—receiving the crown of life.

I am writing this a day after receiving news of the sudden and untimely death of a good friend. In my deep sadness this helps me to hold on to the source of life.

Prayer
Lord Jesus, strengthen those who are suffering today.

ED

Pluralist Pergamum

'This is the message from the one who has a sharp two-edged sword: I know you live in the city where that great throne of Satan is located, and yet you have remained loyal to me. And you have refused to deny me even when Antipas, my faithful witness, was martyred among you by Satan's followers… Everyone who is victorious will eat of the manna that has been hidden away in heaven.'

The city of Pergamum was rife with religion. Paganism was a thriving concern and emperor worship spread from there to many other places. That is the probable meaning of Satan's throne being located in the city. The focus of people's worship, respect and adoration was someone or something other than the God and Father of our Lord Jesus Christ.

The church in the city of Pergamum existed in the midst of a mishmash of beliefs and behaviours. Does that sound familiar? It is exactly the context in which many of us live. In many countries around the world the Church has been marginalised and yet people are still very interested in spirituality. Many in the West have turned to the East to explore other religions in an effort to satisfy their search for meaning and purpose. For some, science has become a religion and atheism has taken on a new popularity. What are Christians to do in this environment?

Jesus commends the church in Pergamum for remaining loyal to him. His message comes from 'the one who has a sharp two-edged sword', an image that represents the truth of God's word (Hebrews 4:12). In the midst of competing religions and persecution, many stayed true to the truth of Jesus and faithful in their relationship with him. How do you maintain your commitment to Jesus when you feel the pull of popular opinion leading you away from him?

Loyalty was rewarded with manna from heaven (Revelation 2:17). This is a reference to the miraculous bread with which God fed his people in the desert (Exodus 16). In John 6:51, Jesus describes himself as the living bread that has come from heaven. The reward for loyalty is more of Jesus himself—now that's what I call nourishment!

Prayer
Lord, give me courage to stay faithful, even when it goes against the tide of popular thinking.

Problems within

'And yet I have a few complaints against you. You tolerate some among you who are like Balaam, who showed Balak how to trip up the people of Israel. He taught them to worship idols by eating food offered to idols and by committing sexual sin. In the same way you have some Nicolaitans among you—people who follow the same teaching and commit the same sins. Repent, or I will come to you suddenly and fight against them with the sword of my mouth.'

We read yesterday of the people in the church at Pergamum who had resisted the pressures from the world around them and stayed loyal to Christ, but there was also a problem and it seems to have been one of compromise within the church. This pressure came from the inside, not the outside. It is likened here to the behaviour of Balaam—a gifted, but maverick prophet in the Old Testament who helped the king of Israel, Balak, to trick God's people (Numbers 22—24). The Nicolaitans (a sect within the Early Church, followers of Nicolaus of Antioch) were guilty of the same sin.

Often the greatest danger to the Church is not external hostility and pressure, but an internal drift away from the truth of the gospel. Notice the inseparable connection between belief and behaviour—false teaching will lead to immoral behaviour. What we believe and how we think determines what we do and how we behave. That is why both are dealt with so regularly in the Bible.

Jesus has stern words for those who are drifting from the truth and getting entangled in immoral behaviour, yet it can be hard to see this drift within ourselves or our churches. One of the key ways to be alert to it seems to revolve around loyalty to Jesus and all that he encapsulates as the truth. That is one of the unique features of Christianity—the truth is personified in Jesus Christ. We do not hold to a philosophy or a code of life but on to our Saviour. To stay close to the truth, we must stay close to Jesus.

Prayer
Lord Jesus, help me be alert to anything that draws me away from worshipping only you, whether that comes from the world or within the Church.

ED

Go for growth

'This is the message from the Son of God, whose eyes are bright like flames of fire, whose feet are like polished bronze: "I know the things you do—your love, your faith, your service and your patient endurance. And I can see your constant improvement in all these things... To all who are victorious, who obey me to the very end, I will give authority over all the nations."'

The penetrating eyes of Jesus are on his church in Thyatira and he sees good as well as bad (we'll deal with the bad tomorrow). As Jesus looked at the Christians in that busy commercial city he saw that they were putting their faith in him into practice in their relationships with one another and in their attitude to the pressures they face to conform to the world around them.

The commendation is not just for the qualities of character that Jesus saw in them but also the fact that they were constantly growing and improving in those areas. Here was a church that was not standing still. They had not succumbed to the complacency that can easily set in and often leads to stagnation.

Whether we apply the challenge of this commendation personally and individually or to a congregation, it is difficult to keep growing. In what ways have you and your church changed in the last year? Are there noticeable improvements in how you are serving one another and the community around you? Are you able to trust God more deeply with an area of your life today than before? Are you growing or stagnating?

Jesus gives an amazing promise here to those who keep going and keep growing—authority over all the nations! How are we to exercise that authority? Jesus said, 'I have been given complete authority in heaven and earth. Therefore, go and make disciples of all the nations' (Matthew 28:18–19). It is quite a thought that he shares his authority over the world with us so that we can introduce other people to him. So often when we are courageous in evangelism we find that we have to depend on Jesus more—and that leads to growth.

Prayer
Help me and my church grow in love, faith, service and endurance.

ED

Consistency is called for

'But I have this complaint against you. You are permitting that woman—that Jezebel who calls herself a prophet—to lead my servants astray. She is encouraging them to worship idols, eat food offered to idols and commit sexual sin. I gave her time to repent, but she would not turn from her immorality.'

There is a split in the church at Thyatira. Not everyone is commended as there are those who have succumbed to the teaching of 'that Jezebel'. John uses the name of the wife of King Ahab here, whose story in the Old Testament is one of seducing God's people away from worshipping him alone. It is Jezebel whom Elijah feared after his showdown with the prophets of Baal (1 Kings 17—19). The likely scenario is that this woman was promoting and encouraging people in the church to be active in the many trade guilds that existed in the city. It was a common way in which business was organised and, to be successful commercially, it was important to be a member of a guild. The problem was that the guilds also involved pagan rituals, sacrifices and worship of the emperor.

The people in the church who were persuaded by this woman's teaching in this way were therefore compromising their faith. In Pergamum, the compromise was a result of people's lives being in danger, but, in Thyatira, it was their livelihoods that were being threatened. Jesus was being worshipped in church, but ignored in business, so what it meant to be a disciple of Jesus was not being consistently applied in every area of life, particularly that of business and commerce.

A friend of mine has a great saying 'Life's a peach, not an orange!' We so easily compartmentalise life, segmenting it like an orange, happily worshipping Christ on a Sunday, but forgetting him and his teaching on a Monday. We are called to consistency—to be the same all the way through, like a peach. Being a Christian must be evident in our working lives as well as in church. Honesty, integrity, justice, mercy, grace and love are qualities that are held in high esteem by Jesus and we are to take these into every area of life. What are the areas of potential inconsistency for you?

Prayer
Lord, help me to stay faithful to you all week.

ED

Reputation isn't everything

'I know all the things you do, and that you have a reputation for being alive—but you are dead. Now wake up! Strengthen what little remains, for even what is left is at the point of death. Your deeds are far from right in the sight of God. Go back to what you heard and believed at first: hold to it firmly and turn to me again. Unless you do, I will come upon you suddenly, as unexpected as a thief.'

All the other messages for the churches have had a bit of good news at the start, but not so the message for Sardis. The city had twice been captured because its people thought their fortress was impregnable and therefore failed to defend it effectively. In Greek folklore it became a classic example of pride before a fall. The church there seemed to be falling into the same trap. From both inside and outside, everything looked fine. They even had a good reputation, but Jesus saw things differently and gave his damning report—he told them that they are dead.

The church had a 'form of godliness, but denied its power' (2 Timothy 3:5). There was a façade but no reality to back it up. They were going through the motions but were deluded. They thought they were fine, but they weren't. Beware good reputations—they don't fool Jesus.

The wider community thought that the church was fine, too. Perhaps they weren't doing anything to upset anyone because they weren't following Jesus rigorously and enthusiastically any more. They had lost their cutting edge and were no longer being effective witnesses.

There are many ways in which we can fall into the same trap. It's not unlike the 'lost love' in the church in Ephesus. What was reality becomes empty. We become concerned with rules rather than gripped by a loving relationship with Jesus. We become so busy going to church meetings that we forget what church is really about.

Jesus urged the church to come back to him—by remembering all that they first heard and believed and repenting, putting him first again. This can remind us of the story that Jesus told elsewhere of the prodigal son (Luke 15). The church in Sardis needed a wake-up call. Jesus, the master of bringing life from death, called them to get back on track.

Prayer

Lord, protect us from false reputations.

ED

Great opportunity

'This is the message from the one who is holy and true. He is the one who has the key of David. He opens doors and no one can shut them; he shuts doors and no one can open them. I know all the things you do, and I have opened a door for you that no one can shut. You have little strength, yet you obeyed my word and did not deny me.'

The letter to the church in Philadelphia (a name meaning 'brotherly love') comes from the great keyholder, the great opener of doors. The city itself had been built in a location that aided the spreading of the Greek language and culture to the barbarian tribes in Phrygia. It was a city with a mission—and the church within it had a mission, too. Jesus is the one who made that mission possible. He holds the key, or the power, to allow people to enter God's kingdom and he is able to open doors of opportunity for that message to reach people's hearts and minds.

The weak church in Philadelphia is praised because it stayed true to Jesus, obeying him and not being afraid to be known as his. Its people showed that they shared in his mission and he reassured them that he is the one who took responsibility for all their mission efforts.

I have often urged student Christian unions to be active in evangelism on campus and the reply will often come, 'We're not ready, we're too small, we don't know enough'. The people of the church in Philadelphia put our excuses to shame as, even in their weakness, they took mission seriously.

As I write this, my church has been doing a special programme of visiting homes in the parish. We have prayed for open doors and open hearts and we have been surprised by some of the doors that have been opened—ones we wouldn't have expected. We rejoice as a congregation that there are people now on the visiting team who were the ones behind the door when we first called a couple of years ago. When Jesus opens a door, it opens wide!

Prayer
Lord Jesus, help me and my church be eager partners in your mission.
Open doors for us, we pray. Amen

ED

REVELATION 3:11–12 (NLT)

Rock solid promises

'Look, I am coming quickly. Hold on to what you have, so that no one will take away your crown. All who are victorious will become pillars in the temple of my God, and they will never have to leave it. And I will write my God's name on them, and they will be citizens in the city of my God—the new Jerusalem that comes down from heaven from my God. And they will have my new name inscribed upon them.'

In 2007 I arrived in Lima, Peru, two days after the earthquake that devastated a large area 120 miles south of the city. Many I spoke with had felt the tremors in the city and described it as a very frightening experience. For those who live in earthquake zones, life is precarious and there is always the fear of disaster. Philadelphia was also in an area subject to frequent earthquakes. By contrast, the promises Jesus made to the Christians there convey stability and permanence.

He promised his personal presence, a victor's crown, a place in the temple of God, a new city and a new name. Imagine how they would have reacted to the thought of being a pillar in God's temple, solid, sure and stable. It's quite a thought for people who often lived outside for fear of the earthquakes. In the New Testament, the temple is used as an image to describe the people of God with his Spirit living in them (1 Corinthians 3:16).

Philadelphia had a few name changes, depending on which emperor was ruling at the time. Jesus promised to give his people God's own name and a new one that no one would know until Jesus came in final victory. His people would be citizens of a new city. Although so much around them was uncertain, unstable and constantly changing, Jesus promised stability. How do you respond to change? How do you react when things take you by surprise? Perhaps you are left feeling insecure and fragile. Be encouraged by all Jesus says: he will bring stability and security beyond anything we can imagine.

Prayer
Through all the changing scenes of life, in trouble and in joy, the praises of my God shall still my heart and tongue employ.

Nahum Tate and Nicholas Brady, 1696
ED

You make me sick!

'I know all the things you do, that you are neither hot nor cold. I wish you were one or the other! But since you are like lukewarm water, I will spit you out of my mouth! You say, "I am rich. I have everything I want. I don't need a thing!" And you don't realise that you are wretched and miserable and poor and blind and naked. I advise you to buy gold from me... Then you will be rich. Also buy white garments [for]... your nakedness, and buy ointment for your eyes so you will be able to see.'

The city of Laodicea was famous for three things: its banks and wealth, its medical expertise, especially in eye ointments, and its clothing industry. This wealthy, self-sufficient city had an embarrassing problem, however—it couldn't sort out a decent water supply. By the time water was channelled from the hot springs nearby to the city, it was lukewarm, not hot enough for washing or healing or cold enough for a refreshing drink.

All these aspects of the city are used by Jesus to criticise the church there. The main problem is that they abandoned Jesus. They had no need of him. They became like the city in which they lived, self-sufficient. They thought that they had it made, that they had all they needed. It made Jesus sick and he revealed the harsh truth to them—in a city famous for wealth, medicine and clothes, the church was poor, blind and naked. In material and economic terms, they may have been rich, but spiritually they were poverty stricken.

In many countries today, it is often hard to preach the gospel because people have no real sense of need. They have everything; life is good. It is sobering to remember that these words were spoken to a church, not to the wider culture. We need to take care that we don't become as self-sufficient as the Christians in Laodicea.

The Church needs Jesus; we cannot do without him. He loves the Church, even in Laodicea, and so invited them to come to him for riches, clothing and good eyesight. What are you relying on in life that holds you back from relying on Jesus for all you need?

Prayer
Lord Jesus, I need you!

ED

REVELATION 3:20–22 (NLT)

Knocking at the door

'Look! Here I stand at the door and knock. If you hear me calling and open the door, I will come in, and we will share a meal as friends. I will invite everyone who is victorious to sit with me on my throne, just as I was victorious and sit with my Father on his throne. Anyone who is willing to hear should listen to the Spirit and understand what the Spirit is saying to the churches.'

We saw yesterday that this self-sufficient church needed Christ himself—and that is what he offered them. He was not just offering resources for their spiritual well-being, he was offering himself. He was knocking for re-admission. Out of love and concern for them, Christ left this church and was on the outside, looking to get back in. This was yet another big wake-up call to the church to see the reality of the dire straits they got themselves into without Christ.

What an offer! He was knocking in order to gain entry as a friend. Sharing a meal is a sign of close friendship and intimacy. This church, which was in danger of being 'spat out' of Jesus' mouth, had been given the opportunity for rescue. Jesus is indeed full of grace, mercy and forgiveness and he longed for them to come to their senses, turn back to him and invite him in.

We may often use this verse in an evangelistic setting, but its context here is for those within the Church, those who call themselves Christians. Jesus is constantly inviting us to put him at the centre of our lives. Will you do that today?

Each message to each church has ended in the same way—if you're willing to hear, listen to the Spirit. Jesus constantly draws us graciously to himself, to the truth of the gospel and all its ramifications. There are severe warnings alongside the rock solid promises, but, as the curtain is drawn back on the realities beyond what we can see, why would we not trust God the Father, Son and Holy Spirit who is the creator and redeemer of the world? We could not be in safer hands.

Prayer

Father God, keep me close to you, enjoying friendship with your Son Jesus and walking in step with your Spirit. Amen

ED

Light in the darkness

As we move from the end of Advent into Christmas proper, our theme is light in the darkness. Of course, the greatest story of light breaking is the incarnation, when God took on human form in the birth of Jesus. We will be engaging with Matthew's crisp account of the birth story, which is the lesser-recounted version (in contrast to Luke's narrative).

Matthew's Gospel has long been the first in the New Testament canon and it forms a solid bridge between the Hebrew Bible (as the Old Testament is now often named) and the New Testament. In the first two chapters alone, Matthew hearkens back to the prophets four times, showing how Jesus is the fulfilment of their prophecies, the longed-for Messiah. He also begins his account with a genealogy that shows clearly how Jesus is God's anointed one.

As we read Matthew's account of Jesus' birth, we see it through Joseph's eyes instead of Mary's (again, as in Luke's). God asked a lot of Joseph and this humble man overcame his incredulity to become the earthly father of the Son of God. Quite often today Joseph is pushed aside or even left out of the Christmas story, but, as we will see, he played a vital role.

We then move on to the first seven of the twelve days of Christmas, during which we will be looking at the theme of light and darkness through the Christian festivals of some of the great saints and martyrs of our faith. It seems paradoxical that, during this time of feasting and joy, we remember Stephen, the first martyr, or the little boys killed by an enraged King Herod, but Jesus was born into a world filled with evil, hatred, gossip and murder; he came to shine his light on this darkness as he ushers in God's kingdom. So, if we are able to celebrate the days of Christmas with joy, we can also pray for those who are trapped in terrible situations, whether poverty, the sex trade, alcoholism, loneliness, broken relationships or other situations.

May the light of the world break through any darkness you are experiencing and may he dispel any gloom as he brings joy, peace and rejoicing. May you also move forward in what is a sometimes cloudy world as you glow with his resplendent light.

Amy Boucher Pye

A Saviour for all

This is the genealogy of Jesus the Messiah the son of David, the son of Abraham: Abraham was the father of Isaac, Isaac the father of Jacob, Jacob the father of Judah and his brothers, Judah the father of Perez and Zerah, whose mother was Tamar, Perez the father of Hezron, Hezron the father of Ram, Ram the father of Amminadab, Amminadab the father of Nahshon, Nahshon the father of Salmon, Salmon the father of Boaz, whose mother was Rahab, Boaz the father of Obed, whose mother was Ruth, Obed the father of Jesse, and Jesse the father of King David. David was the father of Solomon, whose mother had been Uriah's wife.

Did your eyes glaze over as you read this genealogy? So often when reading the Bible we skip over these unfamiliar names. Amminadab? Nahshon? Who are they to me?

There are treasures buried in this list, though, that the original readers would have understood. For instance, unlike most ancient genealogists, Matthew includes women: as well as Mary, Jesus' mother, he names Tamar, Rahab, Ruth and Bathsheba (Uriah's wife). He also includes outcasts (Rahab was a Gentile prostitute), those wronged by men (Tamar had to trick her father-in-law so that he would fulfil his legal obligation for her to marry his son) and those of the 'wrong religion' (as a Moabite, Ruth would have been excluded from the synagogue).

With this, Matthew implies that, although Jesus comes from royal stock (via King David), his roots and very DNA are in those who are marginalised and wronged. As Messiah, he was anointed to save those high in society—and those who were not. Including these so-called questionable women may also be Matthew's way of preparing his readers for the unusual circumstances of Jesus' birth, including that he was born to an unmarried woman.

The way Jesus comes to earth blows apart our preconceptions of how the king of the world should make himself known to his people. He may be high and mighty, but he is also lowly and humble.

Prayer

Lord Jesus Christ, as we prepare to celebrate your coming, open our eyes to those at the margins of society.

ABP

A divine passive

Matthan [was] the father of Jacob, and Jacob the father of Joseph, the husband of Mary, and Mary was the mother of Jesus who is called the Messiah.

What a difference a bit of grammar can make (so says Michael J. Wilkins in *The NIV Application Commentary: Matthew*, Zondervan, 2004). Throughout the genealogy, Matthew has used the Greek verb *gennao* in the active voice, such as 'Abraham fathered Isaac.' After 40 instances of the active verb, he turns here to the passive when describing Mary and Jesus—in the NIV, Joseph was the husband of Mary, 'of whom was born Jesus'. Matthew's readers would have noticed this shift, for it implies what many grammarians 'call a "divine passive", where God is the assumed agent of the action' (p. 63).

In editing classes, our teachers drummed it into us always to use the active voice, but sometimes, as we see here, the passive is quite simply divine. In a simple shift of language, Matthew points to God at work. Watch out, he says, for what comes next is something new and completely different.

When it comes to his people, God is always the divine initiator. Mary responded to him saying yes to God working literally in her body: 'what is conceived in her is from the Holy Spirit' (v. 20). Luke's Gospel records her humble and willing response when the angel announced that she would conceive a child through the 'power of the Most High' (Luke 1:35): 'I am the Lord's servant… may it be to me according to your word' (v. 38). Mary's receptivity changed the world.

How does God want to break through to us today? He may not want us to change the world, but, rather, parts of our world. Perhaps he is opening a new opportunity for service or inviting us to mentor someone or prompting us to extinguish anger and repair a broken relationship. Whatever it is, as we are still and listen for his voice, we will hear his words of love and guidance. May we be as Mary was that day, responding with open hands and a receptive heart.

Reflection

The angel Gabriel said to Mary, 'For no word from God will ever fail'
(Luke 1:37).

ABP

When plans change

This is how the birth of Jesus the Messiah came about: his mother Mary was pledged to be married to Joseph, but before they came together, she was found to be pregnant through the Holy Spirit. Because Joseph her husband was a righteous man and did not want to expose her to public disgrace, he had in mind to divorce her quietly.

The betrothal had taken place and Mary and Joseph were pledged to one another in marriage. Things didn't turn out as they had planned, however, as, before they 'came together' (Matthew's delicate way of implying that they had not had sexual relations), Joseph learned that Mary was expecting a child. At that time, she was probably four months' pregnant, having spent time with her relative Elizabeth, who herself was expecting her son John the Baptist (as we learn in Luke's account).

Courting and marriage were different in biblical times from how they are now. Back then, young men and women would be betrothed to each other for about a year before they entered into marriage. The betrothal would involve exchanging gifts and signing a prenuptial agreement, which gave the man rights over the woman. To break those legal ties entailed divorce. That, then, is what Joseph faced.

Imagine what Joseph was feeling—shocked, angry, hurt, disappointed, indignant, deflated. His plans for spending his life with Mary were shattered. In an instant, everything changed. What was he to do? He could marry her, but that would condone her sin of adultery, leaving him impure before God. He could demand a public divorce, but that would humiliate her publicly and perhaps even result in her death by stoning. He settled on a third option, a private divorce, which would ensure his holiness before God while safeguarding her life.

Your day may be filled with preparations for the feast of Christmas. Stop for a moment, however, to put yourself in Joseph's shoes and forget what comes next in the story. With Joseph, every cell in his body cries out in anguish, 'Why? Why did she? Why me? Why, God? Oh, why?'

Reflection

'As the heavens are higher than the earth, so are my ways higher than your ways and my thoughts than your thoughts' (Isaiah 55:9).

ABP

MATTHEW 1:20–21 (TNIV)

The son of David

> But after he had considered this, an angel of the Lord appeared
> to him in a dream and said, 'Joseph son of David, do not be afraid
> to take Mary home as your wife, because what is conceived in
> her is from the Holy Spirit. She will give birth to a son, and you
> are to give him the name Jesus, because he will save his people
> from their sins.'

After Joseph learned that Mary was pregnant, he despaired about the
future. No doubt she told him about the child's divine origins, but how
could he believe her? Such a story was inconceivable. So, as we saw
yesterday, Joseph chose the best of the unwelcome options—divorce.
God, however, had different plans.

Joseph awoke from his dream and instantly knew the truth of Mary's
pregnancy. The night before, his hopes for marriage had been shattered,
but, in the light of day, he could see a whole new reality shaping up,
including him being the legal father of one who was to become the
Saviour of his people. Surely Joseph woke up a changed man, no longer
despairing but embracing a new life.

When the angel called Joseph 'son of David', it was to establish
Jesus' divine lineage. (Incidentally, Joseph is the only one to be called
a son of David in the New Testament other than Jesus himself.) That
is also why the angel instructed Joseph to name Jesus, for that entails
him formally acknowledging Jesus as his son and, thus, a son of David.
Joseph may not have been the biological father of Jesus, but his role as
his earthly father was vital.

God speaking to his children hasn't changed since biblical times—
he still breaks through, whether in a dream, an insight gleaned from the
Bible, wisdom from friends, our time of prayer or other means. How is
God reaching out to you on this busy day, when you might be finishing
up work or school, buying last-minute presents, preparing food, reading Christmas missives or generally being stressed out? As you go forth,
know that God will speak, even in the midst of all of this.

Prayer

Father, I am busy with many things. Help me to choose what is best.

ABP

The virgin will conceive

All this took place to fulfil what the Lord had said through the prophet: 'The virgin will conceive and give birth to a son...'

Matthew's concise account highlights the miracle of the virgin birth, which was foretold by the prophet Isaiah (7:14). God, through his Holy Spirit, overshadowed Mary and conceived in her Jesus, who is both divine and human. It's a mind-boggling concept of the Trinity at work: God, the creator of the universe, descends through his Holy Spirit to his creation in the person of Jesus, one who is God yet man and, thus, one of the created. Being divine, Jesus can fulfil the meaning of his given name, 'Yahweh saves'. Being human, Jesus can relate to us completely. The whole thing is utterly brilliant.

God didn't stop there, though, for, following Jesus' birth, death and resurrection, there was then Pentecost, when he poured out his Holy Spirit on his people. As the Holy Spirit overshadowed Mary and thus brought about the indwelling of Jesus, we too can host Jesus. Not physically, of course, but Christ living in us transforms us, cleansing us and bringing forth the gifts and fruits of the Spirit (including wisdom, understanding, knowledge, right judgment and love, joy, peace, gentleness, faith and self-control). What better gifts this Christmas season?

Jesus dwelling in us, which is made possible by the incarnation, is echoed in scripture. Jesus referred to it at various times, such as when instructing his disciples before he died ('I am in my Father, and you are in me, and I am in you' in John 14:20) or his final prayer for them ('I in them and you in me' in John 17:23). The apostle Paul reflected this new reality in his letters, such as 'Christ in you, the hope of glory' (Colossians 1:27) or 'I have been crucified with Christ and I no longer live, but Christ lives in me' (Galatians 2:20).

Celebrating the incarnation is a wonderful opportunity to reflect on the reality of Jesus dwelling in us and rejoice.

Prayer

'I pray that out of his glorious riches he may strengthen you with power through his Spirit in your inner being, so that Christ may dwell in your hearts through faith' (Ephesians 3:16–17).

ABP

Messiah, Immanuel, Jesus

'… and they will call him Immanuel' (which means 'God with us').
When Joseph woke up, he did what the angel of the Lord had
commanded him and took Mary home as his wife. But he had no
union with her until she gave birth to a son. And he gave him the
name Jesus.

While Luke's account focuses on Mary and her response to God's work,
Matthew recounts Joseph's willingness to follow God's plans. Joseph
was obedient immediately: he fulfilled the second part of the betrothal,
which was the official marriage ceremony, and he named his son Jesus,
as instructed by the angel.

What's in a name? In biblical times, a name would often connote
characteristics that the parents believed the child would embody. Along
these lines, God, through his angel, told Joseph to name his son Jesus,
which means (as mentioned earlier) 'Yahweh saves' and, as we saw on
Thursday, what Jesus saves his people from is their sins. I don't think
Joseph had any idea of how Jesus would do this, but he welcomed it
from a distance.

Matthew's account also gives Jesus two other names or titles—
Messiah and Immanuel. 'Messiah' is the Hebrew word for one anointed
for a specific task (with 'Christ' being the Greek rendering of this word).
Matthew used this term to signal to his Jewish audience that this was
the coming Saviour, for whom they had been waiting for generations to
bring about God's promised deliverance.

Finally, 'Immanuel' means 'God with us'—God himself took human
form in Jesus. God is with us because Jesus saves us from our sins, for
sin is what separates us from God. Once Jesus rescues us from this
fallen state, we enjoy Immanuel, God with us.

Jesus the anointed one; Jesus who saves; Jesus, God with us. What's
in a name? Simply, it is the whole gospel message.

Prayer

*Lord Jesus, we welcome you this Christmas Day! You are the anointed one,
the God who lives with us, the one who saves. As we praise and worship
you this day, fill us with your presence and love. Help us to reach out to a
world aching to hear your message of good news.*

ABP

The face of an angel

When the members of the Sanhedrin heard this, they were furious and gnashed their teeth at him. But Stephen, full of the Holy Spirit, looked up to heaven and saw the glory of God, and Jesus standing at the right hand of God... At this they covered their ears and, yelling at the top of their voices, they all rushed at him, dragged him out of the city and began to stone him... While they were stoning him, Stephen prayed, 'Lord Jesus, receive my spirit.' Then he fell on his knees and cried out, 'Lord, do not hold this sin against them.'

On this second day of Christmas, as we celebrate Jesus, the light of the world, we also remember Stephen, the first martyr of the faith. He acted as a shaft of light in the darkness surrounding the birth of the Church, as recounted in Acts. He was 'full of God's grace and power, [and] performed great wonders and signs among the people' (Acts 6:8). Some of the Greek-speaking Jews, however, opposed his ministry and called him before the council of the Sanhedrin to give account.

Stephen gave an impassioned speech—the longest recounted in Acts—but what he said incensed the members of the council. When he told of the heavens opening and how he saw Jesus at the right hand of God, their fury reached a climax, for this to them was blasphemy. Covering their ears to protect their purity, they dragged Stephen out of the city and stoned him. As he was dying, Stephen was so filled with the Holy Spirit that he prayed for his murderers and yielded his spirit to the Lord Jesus, just as Jesus did on the cross.

Stephen died dramatically and his martyrdom spread the good news of Jesus exponentially. Martyrdom may not be our calling, but, like Stephen, we can have ready a compelling account of God working in our lives to share as God leads us. As his Holy Spirit fills us, may we, like Stephen, have a face 'like the face of an angel' (6:15).

Prayer

Father God, you have worked throughout history to draw people to yourself. Help me to spread your saving love and truth.

ABP

JOHN 21:19–23 (TNIV, ABRIDGED)

Many parts, one body

Then [Jesus] said to him, 'Follow me!' Peter turned and saw that the disciple whom Jesus loved was following them... When Peter saw him, he asked, 'Lord, what about him?' Jesus answered, 'If I want him to remain alive until I return, what is that to you? You must follow me.' Because of this, the rumour spread among the believers that this disciple would not die. But Jesus did not say that he would not die; he only said, 'If I want him to remain alive until I return, what is that to you?'

Today we celebrate the life and ministry of John, the apostle and evangelist who wrote the Gospel of John, three letters and the book of Revelation. He called himself 'the disciple whom Jesus loved' and was a pillar in the early Church.

He and Peter seemed to have a gentle rivalry, as we can see from our passage today. Jesus had died but hadn't yet ascended to heaven. He had just asked Peter three times if he loved him, restoring Peter after his betrayal of Jesus. Then comes the exchange above. You'd think that Peter would be basking in the assurance of sins forgiven, but, instead, he wonders what is going to happen to John. Specifically, will John be a martyr, too? Jesus here gives a pointed reply: 'You must follow me.' Essentially, he is saying, stop worrying about the others and get on with what I've called *you* to do.

Ever notice how envy strikes when someone in our chosen field succeeds where we haven't? When I was a commissioning editor at a publishing house, two of my colleagues were promoted and I wasn't. I could have echoed Peter, 'What about them, Lord?', but Jesus says to us, 'Follow me.' As we do so, he gives us perspective and heals our wounds. We are all different and, as Bruce Milne says in *The Message of John* (IVP, 1993, p. 319), 'There are many others on the road with us, as truly Christ's, as surely commissioned, as deeply loved, as greatly valued.' May we rejoice in this diversity today.

Reflection
'Dear friends, let us love one another, for love comes from God'
(1 John 4:7).

ABP

MATTHEW 2:13, 16 (TNIV)

The death of innocence

An angel of the Lord appeared to Joseph in a dream. 'Get up,' he said, 'take the child and his mother and escape to Egypt. Stay there until I tell you, for Herod is going to search for the child to kill him.'… When Herod realised that he had been outwitted by the Magi, he was furious, and he gave orders to kill all the boys in Bethlehem and its vicinity who were two years old and under.

As we celebrate the festival of the Holy Innocents today, we return to the story of Jesus' birth and again meet Herod, a jealous, volatile and violent king. Hearing about the new king of the Jews, he wanted to eradicate any potential competition, so, when he realised that the magi were not returning to tell him where Jesus was living as planned, he decided to kill all the little boys in Bethlehem who were two and under. Satisfied, he thought his kingship was secure.

This massacre of around 30 boys (for Bethlehem was a small village) wasn't outside of Herod's character. As Michael Green says in *The Message of Matthew* (IVP, 1988, pp. 70–71), Herod had his wife and her mother killed as well as three of his sons and, when he was dying, he ordered that all the notable men of Jerusalem be killed in the hippodrome.

Herod may have been a powerful king, but his plans to eliminate Jesus were foiled for Joseph was again warned in a dream and he obeyed the angel's direction, trekking into safe territory in Egypt. Clearly our heavenly king was not limited by the wickedness of earthly kings.

Why, though, did those little boys have to die? Why did all those mothers have to weep for their slain children? We just don't know, for it is wrapped up in the fall of humanity and the problem of evil, but we can be certain about God's promises that he will comfort the comfortless and bring hope to the hopeless. We know that he too grieves the loss of children who were so young.

Prayer

Heavenly Father, we don't understand why you sometimes allow innocent people to die. Strengthen our faith and help us to know more of your character.

ABP

Do not be afraid

'Do not be afraid of those who kill the body but cannot kill the soul. Rather, be afraid of the One who can destroy both soul and body in hell. Are not two sparrows sold for a penny? Yet not one of them will fall to the ground outside your Father's care. And even the very hairs of your head are all numbered. So don't be afraid; you are worth more than many sparrows.'

The paradox of feasting while remembering martyrdom continues as we celebrate the life of Thomas Becket. He was named Archbishop of Canterbury in 1162 by King Henry II, to whom he was a chief minister. Henry hoped that by appointing Thomas archbishop he would gain control of the church, but Thomas was as zealous for the church as he had been for the state. Only two years after his appointment, Thomas escaped to France for safety, so incensed was the king over Thomas' exclusion of him from church affairs.

Shortly after Thomas returned to England in 1170, the row intensified even more, with King Henry uttering, 'Who will rid me of this troublesome priest?' Four of his knights decided that that was an order to kill Thomas. They did so as Thomas was taking the service of vespers at Canterbury Cathedral.

Thomas was said to be unafraid in the face of death, echoing Jesus' words to his disciples from Matthew's Gospel. Here Jesus instructs the Twelve as he sends them out to preach the kingdom of God, heal diseases and drive out demons. We may lose our bodies in this world, he says, but what we need to guard against is the one who can kill the body and the soul. We are worth so much more to our Father than even the tiniest of birds, such as a sparrow.

Are you suffering some kind of persecution? If so, may you know the boundless love of the Father as you stand firm against the strategies of the evil one. If not, join me in praying for those around the world who are enduring false accusations or bodily harm because of their faith.

Prayer

*Lord, give us strength to hold on to your promises
in the good times and the bad.*

ABP

MATTHEW 4:12–17 (TNIV, ABRIDGED)

Light and dark

When Jesus heard that John had been put in prison, he... went and lived in Capernaum... to fulfil what was said through the prophet Isaiah: 'Land of Zebulun and land of Naphtali, the Way of the Sea, beyond the Jordan, Galilee of the Gentiles—the people living in darkness have seen a great light; on those living in the land of the shadow of death a light has dawned.' From that time on Jesus began to preach, 'Repent, for the kingdom of heaven has come near.'

On this sixth day of Christmas we don't celebrate any martyrs, but we can continue to meditate on our theme of light and dark. In the passage, we see Jesus beginning his public ministry and Matthew pointing to the fulfilment of Isaiah's prophecy, that those living in darkness would see a great light.

In scripture, darkness implies a place where evil reigns. It nurtures anger, violence, adultery and other sins of the flesh, as well as bitterness, pride, envy, greed and other sins of the spirit. The shadow of death closes in on the living, extinguishing all in its path.

God coming to earth through his son Jesus, however, brings the light that dispels darkness and fear. As David echoes in the Psalms, 'The Lord is my light and my salvation—whom shall I fear?' (27:1). In our fallen world, however, we still have the darkness. Just the other day, our community in North London was rocked by the news of a sexual assault in our local park. 'Never in my 16 years here have I heard of such a thing', said one mother at the school gate. Where people don't know Jesus, darkness will lurk—even in our carefully cultivated public spaces.

We can respond with bitterness or anger or else work to spread Christ's light, pushing back the darkness, bit by bit. As Paul wrote to the church at Thessalonica, 'You are all children of the light and children of the day... Since we belong to the day, let us be sober, putting on faith and love as a breastplate, and the hope of salvation as a helmet' (1 Thessalonians 5:5, 8).

Prayer

Lord Jesus, light of the world, shine in and through me,
that you may dispel the darkness.

ABP

The gift of the Bible

But as for you, continue in what you have learned and have become convinced of, because you know those from whom you learned it, and how from infancy you have known the Holy Scriptures, which are able to make you wise for salvation through faith in Christ Jesus. All Scripture is God-breathed and is useful for teaching, rebuking, correcting and training in righteousness, so that all God's people may be thoroughly equipped for every good work.

Today we remember John Wyclif, the English reformer and Bible translator who died on this day in 1384. He was a Yorkshireman who was educated at Oxford, where he remained for most of his life. He's known as a precursor to the 16th-century Reformation, for he criticised some of the medieval church's doctrines and practices, especially what he considered to be priests meddling between God and his people.

Wyclif wanted people to be able to communicate with God directly, so he initiated a project that translated the Latin Vulgate version of the Bible (the only translation available to him) into English. We think that he translated the Gospels and may have completed as much as the whole New Testament. Those who were opposed to making the Bible available cried out in response, 'The jewel of the clergy has become the toy of the laity.' Clearly, Wyclif's mission was warranted for, as we see in Paul's letter to Timothy, scripture is breathed out of God ('inspired' doesn't have the same weight) and key in equipping the saints for the work of God. Reading the Bible itself won't bring us salvation, but, as Paul says, it can make us wise for salvation through faith in Jesus.

Tomorrow, you may wish to make a resolution for 2011. One sound undertaking is to commit to spending time with God's word. We can thank visionary believers such as Wyclif for the access we have to our own copies of the Bible, while also supporting the work of Bible societies and translators, who are fighting Bible poverty worldwide.

Prayer

Lord, thank you for the gift of your scriptures. Help us to take, read and inwardly digest them, that we might be equipped for your service.

ABP

The BRF

Magazine

Richard Fisher writes...

'Give up the ghost', 'out of the mouths of babes and sucklings', 'the writing's on the wall', 'the powers that be', 'the spirit is willing, but the flesh is weak', 'the blind leading the blind'... all of these phrases are in common usage today, but did you know that they come straight from the King James Version of the Bible, first published in 1611? Next year marks its 400th anniversary and exciting plans have been developing over the past two years to make 2011 a year of celebration of the Bible in the English language. The celebrations have two core strands.

The 2011 Trust (www.2011trust.org) is focusing on the arts, heritage and education, and as a result a wide range of initiatives will be taking place throughout the year—including conferences, lectures, exhibitions and celebrations of the Bible in art, music and film. BRF's particular involvement will be with primary schools, providing a new In-Service Training session for teachers on using the Bible with children in the classroom, and a new version of our creative arts-based Barnabas RE Day theme, 'What's so special about the Bible?'

The second strand is 'Biblefresh' (www.biblefresh.com), a multi-organisation collaboration led by the Evangelical Alliance, intended to stimulate and resource churches to engage afresh with the Bible and its message. You can read more about it on the following pages.

We'd like to hear your stories and reflections. What does the Bible mean to you? How has it influenced your life? Is there a particular Bible verse or passage that is significant to you? Would you be willing to share this with us? Are there particular books or resources that have helped you in your reading and exploration of the Bible, which you'd like to commend to others? During 2011 we'd like to collect these stories and comments and publish them on our website. Your own experiences and insights could be a great help and inspiration to others.

We're excited by the way so many organisations and individuals are supporting the plans for 2011, and we encourage you and your church to get involved too. Who knows what an impact this might have?

Richard Fisher, Chief Executive

Biblefresh

Rob Cotton

It could change your world

Knowledge of the Bible seems to be vanishing fast in the UK, according to a recent Durham University survey. A bemused 60 per cent of the general public couldn't recall anything about the parable of the good Samaritan, and a third of under-45s (for whom Bible awareness seemed weakest) scratched their heads to remember anything about the feeding of the five thousand.

Against this background, perhaps it's unsurprising that Christians, too, face increasing difficulties in engaging with the Bible—but an exciting new campaign is aiming to reverse the trend.

The campaign 'Biblefresh' will encourage people to take another look at the Bible, to engage with scripture in ways that will transform their relationship with the Bible, enabling real experiences of spiritual renewal.

As Bible Society's Senior Campaign Manager, I have been seconded to Evangelical Alliance as the Network Coordinator for Biblefresh, to envision churches and organisations. I am genuinely excited about Biblefresh and the opportunity to mobilise churches in discovering fresh approaches that bring release from any sense of guilt or failure, and aid new understanding. God still speaks through his word today.

Biblefresh begins in churches preparing themselves in prayer during Advent this year and will climax in a year-long campaign in 2011—all with the aim of giving Christians a new confidence and excitement about using scripture. 2011 is the 400th anniversary of the King James Version of the Bible. This has provided a focus for the campaign, which is currently gathering real momentum, with the Methodist Church nationally designating 2011 'Biblefresh—The year of the Bible' and other denominations and networks doing the same.

It is important that churches launch Biblefresh effectively in the new year, inviting church members to covenant to engage with the Bible in new ways during the year. There will be high points of the campaign around the Christian festivals, focusing upon 'the Cross' at Easter, 'Communication' to people in their own heart language at Pentecost and 'Carnivals' over the summer, 'Cultivation' of God's word throughout the season of harvest, and finally 'Christmas' as the climax of the year.

Some 50 Christian agencies and colleges are already behind the Evangelical Alliance-led initiative, with BRF, Bible Society, Scripture Union and Wycliffe Bible translators among the key partners. But it is important that those who love scripture and engage with its life-changing message make the most of the opportunities during the Biblefresh campaign to share the word of God with others and invite them to share in the Bible experiences.

The campaign will offer churches four streams of involvement. These are Bible reading (new publications are being developed and public reading events are being organised), Bible training (with major festivals already preparing to offer a programme in keeping with the campaign, courses and Bible boot camps), Bible translation (into our 21st-century culture as well as languages around the world) and Bible experience (using film, music, drama, fine arts and exhibitions). The specially designed website www.biblefresh.com will keep churches updated with the latest campaign news and resources, and a further website, www.2011trust.org, gives information on civic events and arts initiatives.

… to share the word of God with others…

There have already been some significant events to prepare the church for Biblefresh, in two envisioning tours with musicians Paul Field and Dan Wheeler, plus Australian band Sons of Korah, who have creatively set the Psalms to music. The Sons of Korah's impact, singing scripture to an audience, has been amazing to see, and no doubt their tour will be a highlight of the Biblefresh campaign.

Biblefresh will enable organisations to profile their resources, and readers can look forward to new and exciting initiatives that will encourage, challenge and renew their passion for the word of God.

Envisioning events have given church leaders the full picture to pass on to their congregations, and the events have featured well-known Bible champions who are supporting the campaign. There is also a resources handbook for churches, to envision leaders and church members to make the most of Biblefresh. This handbook is a must-read publication.

'Biblefresh: It could change your world'—your personal world or the wider world, as people apply the message to their lives.

For further information, contact Revd Rob Cotton (rob.cotton@biblesociety.org.uk; Tel: 07766 075486) or Alexandra Lilley (a.lilley@eauk.org; Tel: 020 7207 2109)

The Revd Rob Cotton is Senior Campaign Manager at the Bible Society

An interview with Heather Fenton

Heather Fenton is a priest in the Church in Wales and has run the retreat house, Coleg y Groes , for 25 years. In September 2009 she became editor of *Quiet Spaces*, BRF's prayer and spirituality journal. Rachel Walker, BRF's Marketing Coordinator, spoke to Heather and asked her about her life and how she came to be editing *Quiet Spaces*.

How did you get to where you are today?
I became a Christian when I was 15, although, like many children in the early 1960s, I had some residual Christian faith before that, and had been confirmed because there were classes at the independent school at which I was a 'day girl'. I was in the Youth Fellowship at the local village church in west Kent, and when I became a Christian I joined the choir as an excuse for going to church. About 18 months later, I had an experience of the baptism of the Holy Spirit, which was very controversial at the time, and over which I had quite a hard time.

Early on, I realised that God had a special calling for each one of us, and I looked round to see what that might be for me. As I was good at art, I decided that perhaps I should go to art school. So this is what I did when I left school, and that's how I got into my career in publishing.

While at art school, I specialised in lettering (hand-drawn lettering is my speciality, although I don't do much at the moment) and typography. Afterwards I worked for publishers, including Routledge and OUP, initially producing their publicity material but going on to work in their Production Departments. As I wanted to have a better theological understanding, I began to think and pray about going to theological college. In 1976 I was made redundant and took the opportunity to go to Trinity College in Bristol to study theology. I then went back into publishing for another eight years, and ended up as a Production Manager. It was then that God moved me to rural Wales and, together with some friends, I set up the retreat house Coleg y Groes. This is now in its 25th year and has been used by God for a great many people during that time.

Where is your ministry based?
I was ordained in the Church in Wales as a deacon in 1987 and as a priest ten years later. I have served in a number of parishes in this remote rural deanery over the last 23 years. At the time of writing, I am vicar of two rural parishes, small in number and massive in terms of area. They are Welsh-speaking sheep-farming areas. I am well known for my innovative worship services and my work with primary school-age children, and am a school chaplain as well as a governor.

What is your current role in publishing?
I have helped the Church in Wales with the production of some of their publications. I am currently Editor of the Church of England magazine for Lay Readers (licensed lay ministers) called *The Reader* and have been appointed as the new editor of *Quiet Spaces*. This latter role brings together my experience in running a retreat house with my long career in publishing. I always think God is good at making the best use of resources!

> *God is good at making the best use of resources*

What have been the main influences on your own spiritual journey?
The evangelical wing of the Anglican church, plus the charismatic movement (Fountain Trust, for example), as well as the Fisherfolk and the associated community movement, which started at the Church of the Holy Redeemer in Houston, Texas, and spread to the UK (Cumbrae in Scotland and Post Green in Dorset) in the 1960s and '70s, were all very influential for me. Now I am a founder member of quite a small dispersed community, 'The Community of Coleg y Groes', associated with the retreat house ministry I have had for the last 24 years. Ten years ago I took an MA in Celtic Christianity, which was very stimulating and a great blessing.

What are you hoping to do in the future?
I am planning to retire from parish work and to sell Coleg y Groes, but to stay in Wales. I will be working for the Church of England and BRF, and may well produce some publications of my own. I also want to do some more art, especially using texture and lettering images, and I have a vegetable patch.

Heather Fenton is editor of Quiet Spaces *and a priest in the Church in Wales. This year's issues of* Quiet Spaces *are entitled 'Yesterday', 'Today' and 'Tomorrow'.*

The People's Bible

Martyn Payne

As you will have read elsewhere in this issue, Christians are gearing up for a big celebration next year. 2011 marks the 400th anniversary of the publication of the Authorised (King James) Bible—the Bible in the language of the people—which has had such a radical impact on the life and culture of our nation and, through the work of missionaries and the expansion of the British Empire, on the whole world. The Barnabas Children's Ministry team is not going to miss out on this moment! Plans are well under way to use the anniversary as a springboard for our work in primary schools across the UK in 2011.

In the course of the last decade, Barnabas in Schools has become a respected and valued partner in support of the teaching of Religious Education in our primary schools. Well over 800 of our unique RE Days have been enjoyed by thousands of children as we have endeavoured to explore Christianity creatively and opened up the Bible with mime, drama, music, dance and various storytelling styles. Building on this platform, BRF and the Barnabas children's team have been working with the 2011 Trust and will be taking a lead in the delivery of some specially designed RE Days; these days will help children to unpack both the spiritual and the cultural legacy of the King James Bible. We have also been given funding to offer INSET sessions for teachers to Anglican dioceses in the country, which will explore the story of the Bible and look at creative ways to share it with children. This God-given opportunity is a very exciting project indeed, and one that the Barnabas children's team, with its experience and proven track record, is well placed to deliver.

> *Over 800 of our unique RE Days have been enjoyed by thousands of children*

To pick up a copy of the Authorised Version of the Bible and open its double-columned pages may not seem like anything special to us today, but 400 years ago, in 1611, doing just this was nothing short of a revolution. It opened up a whole new world of possibilities and led to changes in thinking that shaped the course of history and the culture of the Western world. This one book has left a lasting legacy, right up to the present day.

Just imagine. Being able to read the Bible in your own language, English, in 1611 was like… the first time our generation logged on to the Internet: suddenly a whole new world of information and ideas was at its fingertips. It was like… the first time our generation used an iPhone to speak to and even see friends and relatives overseas: suddenly a whole new world of communications and contacts was available. It was like… the first time our generation, while watching live TV, was able to influence the outcome of events by pressing a red button: suddenly a whole new world of influence and power could be accessed by ordinary men and women, who until then had received everything second-hand and at a disabling distance. So you can see why this anniversary is well worth celebrating!

> *God's words in the Authorised Version leapt off the page and had a profound impact*

Alongside the special RE Days and INSET sessions, a resource book called *The People's Bible* will be published by Barnabas, including the background story to the publication of the King James Bible and its influence, as well as suggestions for classroom activities. There are also plans to produce a DVD of members of our team demonstrating some of the lesson ideas.

There is always, of course, the danger that an anniversary like this might end up just looking backwards. But although it is right and proper to mark this significant historical moment, when that moment has to do with the living word of God, there is no way it can remain as history. God's words in the Authorised Version leapt off the page and had a profound impact on the lives and culture of the people of that day. As Christians, we believe that this still can be true today. The challenge for the Barnabas ministry team is to present children with Bible stories that are not just for then but for *them*!

The 'for ever' but also 'for now' dimension of the words of scripture is very familiar to the Barnabas children's ministry team is very familiar. Our aim has always been to take the 'timeless' truths of the Bible and find creative ways to make them 'timely' for the children. Children do not suffer religious language or disconnected learning gladly, so we have always needed to make the Bible relevant to our own time and culture, just as the brave translators 400 years ago did when they approached the Greek and Latin manuscripts before them. What miracles happened then, and still do happen, when we let scripture breathe like this! As a team, we have lost count of the number of times children's responses on our RE Days have taken us by surprise, revealing new insights into the stories as well as reminding us of a child's God-given gift to the church—namely, to teach us how to enter the kingdom of God. All of you who have ever worked with children have, I am sure, had the same experiences.

> *A child's God-given gift to the church— to teach us how to enter the kingdom of God*

Celebrating the impact of *The People's Bible* with primary school children and their teachers next year will be a privilege. Do pray for us as we introduce them to the Bible—a Book of Books that is not only a window into God's work with people in the past, but also a mirror in which we can discover God at work with us today.

For more information about *The People's Bible* and the special RE Days for children and INSET for teachers in 2011, please contact Lynda Ward, the Barnabas Team Administrator: barnabas@brf.org.uk; tel: 01865 319704.

Martyn Payne is a member of the Barnabas children's ministry team, based in London.

Recommended reading

Naomi Starkey

Time and again, we hear media reports about today's anonymous society, in which no one looks out for their neighbour or feels any sense of responsibility for what goes on beyond their front door. For better or worse, a church or chapel building is a highly visible symbol of people coming together for a common purpose.

People come along to their local church for a variety of reasons. Of course, it is often because they are already Christians and want a place where they can worship—or they may be seeking God and (rightly) reckon that attending a church service is a good starting point. More than a few, however, come in search of a sense of belonging, some kind of community, and this search may not necessarily be linked to an active faith. As a result, it creates tremendous opportunities for witness and ministry but also great responsibilities in terms of pastoral care.

In *Growing a Caring Church*, Wendy Billington draws on her years of pastoral work in the community and in the local church, to share ways in which Christians can not only care for one another but also extend this care to people in the wider neighbourhood. Her role as coordinator of the pastoral care programme in a large church includes providing training in pastoral skills, listening to people's concerns, bereavement care, marriage enrichment and supporting cancer sufferers and their families.

When leadership resources are already stretched, pastoral care is an area in which it is all too easy to fall short, with potentially disastrous consequences. And if a church cannot nurture its own members, how can it hope to be strong enough to care for anyone else? Aware of this challenge, Wendy shows how church home groups can be places where people's pain and difficulties are noticed, and first steps are taken to help. Following Jesus' command that as his disciples we are to love one another and also share his love with the world, we can learn how to offer the kind of wise and practical assistance that will start to guide those who are struggling back towards wholeness of life.

A crucial skill in all kinds of pastoral care is the art of listening, something that is in danger of being lost in our noisy, stressed and superficial world. We forget about listening not only to others but also to God, to ourselves, to our communities—and even to the needs of our planet. If we do not listen, we cannot hope to grow in wisdom, to deepen relationships with others or to share our faith in sensitive and appropriate ways.

BRF are pleased to be publishing a new edition of Michael Mitton's *A Heart to Listen*, which explores how, with God's help, we can relearn this essential art. Michael interweaves biblical reflection with insights from many years of listening ministry in the UK and abroad. To speak to heart as well as head, he concludes each chapter with an episode from a creative story that tells of people listening and learning from one another in a challenging crosscultural setting.

Now a freelance writer and consultant, Michael headed up the Christian Listeners ministry of the Acorn Christian Healing Foundation (where he was also deputy director) for a number of years, before working as Diocesan Mission and Ministry Development Adviser for Derby diocese. He has also written *A Handful of Light* and *Restoring the Woven Cord* (new edition) for BRF, and is a contributor to *New Daylight* Bible reading notes.

He wrote *A Heart to Listen* not only because of his belief in the importance of this skill for every area of Christian discipleship but also to encourage people to take first steps in developing it for themselves. In his preface for the new edition, he shares something of the reaction he has received to the book, including an email about its effect on one reader: 'She wrote, "I want to say thank you for your wonderful but disturbing book. It made me weep and laugh out loud; it gave me such hope and joy. A lot of changes are happening at our local church and not without much heartache and soul-searching. Your book has given me confidence to see things through with the grace of our Lord and the love and compassion that he has given me for people."'

> *Learning to listen draws us into the heart of God*

He continues: 'On the days when I struggle with confidence and wish I was a better writer, I go back to emails like this and realise that something of my message has actually got through in this book. The message is essentially very simple: learning to listen draws us into the heart of God, to feel something of the compassion and care that he feels for the humans he has created. When we encounter this, it affects everything.'

To order a copy of any of these books, please turn to page 159.

Pilgrims TO THE MANGER

NAOMI STARKEY

A daily journey through Advent to Epiphany

THE BRF ADVENT BOOK

An extract from *Pilgrims to the Manger*

BRF's Advent book for 2010, written by *New Daylight* editor Naomi Starkey, is an invitation to a pilgrimage through Advent, Christmas and Epiphany. In the following extract, the Introduction to the book, Naomi explains the imagery on which the book is based and offers us both refreshment and challenge as we take up the invitation to journey with her.

'Christmas isn't what it used to be!' I was twelve years old, sitting on my bed, tears trickling down my cheeks as I gazed out in a melodramatic verge-of-adolescence way at the rooftops of suburban Cambridge. My mother hovered in the doorway, trying to make sense of my mood amid the 1001 tasks of a family Christmas Eve.

While I had known for years that there was no Father Christmas (although I pretended, to keep my younger siblings happy), what triggered my despair was finding that I no longer felt the magic. *I wasn't excited any more.* I knew the stories of baby Jesus inside out and back to front; I was still up and about when my mother was filling the stockings; I knew that Christmas dinner was followed by mountains of washing up. I would go to bed on 24 December, wake up next morning and, yes, there would be presents—but in the end it was just another day, followed by the next, and the next.

Thankfully, life has moved on in all kinds of ways since then. I have come to realise the difference between knowing Bible stories and understanding their message; I have learned the pleasures of giving as well as receiving; I have discovered the blessed invention that is the dishwasher. When my own daughter was born at the end of November one year, she appeared as the Christmas morning sermon illustration—and I found that all the carols about mother and baby acquired special resonance.

Christmases continue to come and go, though, and each year the turn of the seasons seems to happen faster. The round-robin letters, which I for one always enjoy, start to change. Instead of announcing the latest baby, music exam grade or Brownie badge, the news is of children starting to scatter from the family home to further education, jobs or travel. For my parents' generation, there is the shock of familiar names beginning to disappear from the Christmas card list, couples of names dwindling to one on its own. The letters are increasingly dominated by health issues and the upheavals of retirement and downsizing.

It may be, too, that as we try to sum up our news for family and friends, we face the uncomfortable truth that life hasn't turned out quite as we expected. Somehow or other, we never did get that promotion. Yes, our marriage held together but we keep thinking about that old flame we met at the school reunion. Thanks to the economic climate, our dreams of trading up to a more commodious house have evaporated, at least for now. Then there's our relationship with God. Yes, we go to a lovely church but somehow the worship doesn't touch us in the same way any more. Same old hymns, same old Bible readings, same old sermons that leave us feeling vaguely—or sometimes specifically—guilty. And, dare we say it to ourselves, 'Same old God'?

This book of readings is an invitation to pilgrimage, to accompany me through the weeks of Advent, to Christmas itself and on to Epiphany. As the days and weeks pass, we will reflect together on a range of issues—the significance of the festivities, the deeper values that underpin our lives, some of the other special days in the Church calendar at this season, and how we can begin to deepen our understanding of God's perspective on our world, our church and ourselves.

> *A pilgrimage of both head and heart*

'Pilgrimage' is more than a figure of speech in this book, however. I invite you to join an imaginary group of pilgrims whose path takes them from a city centre high street, out to the suburbs, beyond the city to a mountain top (don't worry—it's not very high), and then back into the city to find the cathedral, where we rest for the celebrations surrounding Christmas Day itself. In the following days, we travel beyond the streets and down to the sea, where this book concludes. It's not a conventional pilgrimage. It does not follow a well-trodden route to a well-known destination, although we will pass familiar landmarks; it is a pilgrimage of both head and heart in that our aim is to learn more of God and allow ourselves to be challenged by what we discover as we journey together. Above all, we will discover the truth of Immanuel: God is here, everywhere, present with us, if only we will look up and notice him walking alongside us.

Naomi Starkey is Commissioning Editor for BRF's adult list and edits and writes for New Daylight. *She has also written* Good Enough Mother *for BRF. To order either of her books, please turn to the order form on page 159.*

New Daylight © BRF 2010

The Bible Reading Fellowship
15 The Chambers, Vineyard, Abingdon OX14 3FE
Tel: 01865 319700; Fax: 01865 319701
E-mail: enquiries@brf.org.uk; Website: www.brf.org.uk

ISBN 978 1 84101 556 9

Distributed in Australia by Willow Connection, PO Box 288, Brookvale, NSW 2100.
Tel: 02 9948 3957; Fax: 02 9948 8153;
E-mail: info@willowconnection.com.au
Available also from all good Christian bookshops in Australia.
For individual and group subscriptions in Australia:
Mrs Rosemary Morrall, PO Box W35, Wanniassa, ACT 2903.

Distributed in New Zealand by Scripture Union Wholesale, PO Box 760, Wellington
Tel: 04 385 0421; Fax: 04 384 3990; E-mail: suwholesale@clear.net.nz

Publications distributed to more than 60 countries

Acknowledgments
The New Revised Standard Version of the Bible, Anglicized Edition, copyright © 1989, 1995 by the
Division of Christian Education of the National Council of the Churches of Christ in the USA.
Used by permission. All rights reserved.

The Holy Bible, New International Version, copyright © 1973, 1978, 1984, 1995 by International
Bible Society. Used by permission of Hodder & Stoughton Publishers, a member of the
Hachette Livre UK Group. All rights reserved. 'NIV' is a registered trademark of International
Bible Society. UK trademark number 1448790.

The Holy Bible, Today's New International Version, copyright © 2004 by International Bible
Society. Used by permission of Hodder & Stoughton Publishers, a member of the Hachette
Livre UK Group. All rights reserved. 'TNIV' is a registered trademark of International Bible
Society.

The Holy Bible, New Living Translation, copyright © 1996, 2004. Used by permission of Tyndale
House Publishers, Inc., Wheaton, Illinois 60189. All rights reserved.

Extracts from the Authorised Version of the Bible (The King James Bible), the rights in which
are vested in the Crown, are reproduced by permission of the Crown's Patentee, Cambridge
University Press.

The Revised Common Lectionary is copyright © The Consultation on Common Texts, 1992 and is
reproduced with permission. *The Christian Year: Calendar, Lectionary and Collects*, which includes
the *Common Worship* lectionary (the Church of England's adaptations of the *Revised Common
Lectionary*, published as the Principal Service lectionary) is copyright © The Central Board
of Finance of the Church of England, 1995, 1997, and material from it is reproduced with
permission.

Printed in Singapore by Craft Print International Ltd

SUPPORTING BRF'S MINISTRY

As a Christian charity, BRF is involved in five distinct yet complementary areas.

- **BRF** (www.brf.org.uk) resources adults for their spiritual journey through Bible reading notes, books, and a programme of quiet days and teaching days. BRF also provides the infrastructure that supports our other four specialist ministries.
- **Foundations21** (www.foundations21.org.uk) provides flexible and innovative ways for individuals and groups to explore their Christian faith and discipleship through a multimedia internet-based resource.
- **Messy Church**, led by Lucy Moore (www.messychurch.org.uk), enables churches all over the UK (and increasingly abroad) to reach children and adults beyond the fringes of the church .
- **Barnabas in Churches** (www.barnabasinchurches.org.uk) helps churches to support, resource and develop their children's ministry with the under-11s more effectively .
- **Barnabas in Schools** (www.barnabasinschools.org.uk) enables primary school children and teachers to explore Christianity creatively and bring the Bible alive within RE and Collective Worship.

At the heart of BRF's ministry is a desire to equip adults and children for Christian living—helping them to read and understand the Bible, to explore prayer and to grow as disciples of Jesus. We need your help to make a real impact on the local church, local schools and the wider community.

- You could support BRF's ministry with a donation or standing order (using the response form overleaf).
- You could consider making a bequest to BRF in your will.
- You could encourage your church to support BRF as part of your church's giving to home mission—perhaps focusing on a specific area of our ministry, or a particular member of our Barnabas team.
- Most important of all, you could support BRF with your prayers.

If you would like to discuss how a specific gift or bequest could be used in the development of our ministry, please phone 01865 319700 or email enquiries@brf.org.uk.

Whatever you can do or give, we thank you for your support.

BRF MINISTRY APPEAL RESPONSE FORM

Name _____

Address _____

_____ Postcode _____

Telephone _____ Email _____
(tick as appropriate)

Gift Aid Declaration

❑ I am a UK taxpayer. I want BRF to treat as Gift Aid Donations all donations I make from 6 April 2000 until I notify you otherwise.

Signature _____ Date _____

❑ I would like to support BRF's ministry with a regular donation by standing order (please complete the Banker's Order below).

Standing Order – Banker's Order

To the Manager, Name of Bank/Building Society

Address _____

_____ Postcode _____

Sort Code _____ Account Name _____

Account No _____

Please pay Royal Bank of Scotland plc, Drummonds, 49 Charing Cross, London SW1A 2DX (Sort Code 16-00-38), for the account of BRF A/C No. 00774151

The sum of _____ pounds on ___ /___ /___ (insert date your standing order starts) and thereafter the same amount on the same day of each month until further notice.

Signature _____ Date _____

Single donation

❑ I enclose my cheque/credit card/Switch card details for a donation of £5 £10 £25 £50 £100 £250 (other) £ _____ to support BRF's ministry

Credit/Switch card no. ☐☐☐☐ ☐☐☐☐ ☐☐☐☐ ☐☐☐☐

Expires ☐☐☐☐ Security code ☐☐☐ Issue no. (Switch only) ☐☐☐☐

Signature _____ Date _____
(Where appropriate, on receipt of your donation, we will send you a Gift Aid form)

❑ Please send me information about making a bequest to BRF in my will.

Please detach and send this completed form to: Richard Fisher, BRF, 15 The Chambers, Vineyard, Abingdon OX14 3FE. BRF is a Registered Charity (No.233280)

ND 0310

BIBLE READING RESOURCES PACK

An updated pack of resources and ideas to help to promote Bible reading in your church is available from BRF. The pack, which will be of use at any time during the year (but especially for Bible Sunday in October), includes sample readings from BRF's Bible reading notes and *The People's Bible Commentary*, and lots of ideas for promoting Bible reading in your church.

Unless you specify the month in which you would like the pack sent, we will send it immediately on receipt of your order. The pack is free if despatched to a UK address (but if you would like to make a donation towards the cost, we will greatly appreciate it). If you require a pack sent outside the UK, please contact us and we will quote for postage and packing. We welcome your comments about the contents of the pack and your ideas for future ones.

This coupon should be sent to:

BRF
15 The Chambers
Vineyard
Abingdon
OX14 3FE

Name _____

Address _____

_____

_____ Postcode _____

Telephone _____

Email _____

Please send me _____ Bible Reading Resources Pack(s)

Please send the pack now/ in _____ (month).

I enclose a donation for £ _____ towards the cost of the pack.

BRF is a Registered Charity

SUBSCRIPTIONS

❏ Please send me a Bible reading resources pack
❏ I would like to take out a subscription myself (complete your name and address details only once)
❏ I would like to give a gift subscription (please complete both name and address sections below)

Your name _____

Your address _____

_____ Postcode _____

Tel _____ Email _____

Gift subscription name _____

Gift subscription address _____

_____ Postcode _____

Gift message (20 words max.) _____

Please send *New Daylight* beginning with the January / May / September 2011 issue: (delete as applicable)

(please tick box)	UK	SURFACE	AIR MAIL
NEW DAYLIGHT	❏ £14.40	❏ £15.90	❏ £19.20
NEW DAYLIGHT 3-year sub	❏ £36.00		
NEW DAYLIGHT DELUXE	❏ £18.00	❏ £22.50	❏ £28.80
NEW DAYLIGHT daily email only	❏ £12.00 (UK and overseas)		
NEW DAYLIGHT email + printed	❏ £23.40	❏ £24.90	❏ £28.20

Confirm your email address _____

Please complete the payment details below and send, with appropriate payment, to: **BRF, 15 The Chambers, Vineyard, Abingdon OX14 3FE.**

Total enclosed £ _____ (cheques should be made payable to 'BRF')

Please charge my Visa ❏ Mastercard ❏ Switch card ❏ with £ _____

Card number ☐☐☐☐☐☐☐☐☐☐☐☐☐☐☐☐☐☐☐☐

Expires ☐☐☐☐ Security code ☐☐☐ Issue no (Switch only) ☐☐☐☐

Signature (essential if paying by credit/Switch) _____

BRF is a Registered Charity

ND 0310

BRF PUBLICATIONS ORDER FORM

Please ensure that you complete and send off both sides of this order form.
Please send me the following book(s):

		Quantity	Price	Total
709 9	Pilgrims to the Manger (N. Starkey)	_____	£7.99	_____
612 2	Good Enough Mother (N. Starkey)	_____	£5.99	_____
799 0	Growing a Caring Church (W. Billington)	_____	£6.99	_____
747 1	A Heart to Listen (M. Mitton)	_____	£8.99	_____
800 3	Restoring the Woven Cord (M. Mitton)	_____	£8.99	_____
247 6	A Handful of Light (M. Mitton)	_____	£7.99	_____
503 3	Messy Church (L. Moore)	_____	£8.99	_____
725 9	Countdown to Christmas with Timothy Bear (B. Sears)	_____	£6.99	_____
821 8	Ten Little Sheep (J. Godfrey)	_____	£6.99	_____
822 5	Joseph's Story of Christmas (G. Guadagno)	_____	£5.99	_____
659 7	Quiet Spaces: Yesterday (H. Fenton)	_____	£4.99	_____
660 3	Quiet Spaces: Today (H. Fenton)	_____	£4.99	_____
661 0	Quiet Spaces: Tomorrow (H. Fenton) (avail. November)	_____	£4.99	_____
027 4	PBC: Luke (H. Wansbrough)	_____	£7.99	_____
151 6	PBC: Isaiah (J. Bailey Wells)	_____	£8.99	_____
118 9	PBC: 1 & 2 Kings (S.B. Dawes)	_____	£7.99	_____
047 2	PBC: Ephesians to Colossians and Philemon (M. Maxwell)	_____	£7.99	_____

Total cost of books £ _____

Donation £ _____

Postage and packing £ _____

TOTAL £ _____

POSTAGE AND PACKING CHARGES				
order value	UK	Europe	Surface	Air Mail
£7.00 & under	£1.25	£3.00	£3.50	£5.50
£7.01–£30.00	£2.25	£5.50	£6.50	£10.00
Over £30.00	free	prices on request		

For more information about new books and special offers, visit www.brfonline.org.uk. See over for payment details. All prices are correct at time of going to press, are subject to the prevailing rate of VAT and may be subject to change without prior warning.

PAYMENT DETAILS

Please complete the payment details below and send with appropriate payment and completed order form to:

BRF, 15 The Chambers, Vineyard, Abingdon OX14 3FE

Name _____

Address _____

_____ Postcode _____

Telephone _____

Email _____

Total enclosed £ _____ (cheques should be made payable to 'BRF')

Please charge my Visa ❏ Mastercard ❏ Switch card ❏ with £_____

Card number: ⬜⬜⬜⬜⬜⬜⬜⬜⬜⬜⬜⬜⬜⬜⬜⬜⬜⬜⬜

Expires ⬜⬜⬜⬜ Security code ⬜⬜⬜ Issue no (Switch only) ⬜⬜⬜⬜

Signature (essential if paying by credit/Switch) _____

❏ Please do not send me further information about BRF publications.

ALTERNATIVE WAYS TO ORDER

Christian bookshops: All good Christian bookshops stock BRF publications. For your nearest stockist, please contact BRF.

Telephone: The BRF office is open between 09.15 and 17.30. To place your order, phone 01865 319700; fax 01865 319701.

Web: Visit www.brf.org.uk

ND 0310